IN SILENCIO ET SPE ERIT ... FORTITVDO VESTRA

*P*ORTRAIT *of MARTIN LUTHER*
By Cranach.   Original in Milan.

CONVERSATIONS WITH LUTHER

Selections from recently published sources
of the

TABLE TALK

Translated and edited
by

PRESERVED SMITH, Ph.D.

Author of "The Life and Letters of Martin Luther," etc., editor of
"Luther's Correspondence and other
contemporary Letters," etc.

AND

HERBERT PERCIVAL GALLINGER, Ph.D.

Associate Professor of History at Amherst College

KEATS PUBLISHING, INC.
NEW CANAAN, CONNECTICUT

CONVERSATIONS WITH LUTHER

Shepherd Illustrated Classic edition published 1979

Special contents copyright © 1979 by
Keats Publishing, Inc.

Library of Congress Catalog Card Number: 79-64830
ISBN: 0-87983-209-6

Printed in the United States of America

SHEPHERD ILLUSTRATED CLASSICS are published
by Keats Publishing, Inc.
36 Grove Street, New Canaan, Connecticut 06840

CONTENTS

CONTENTS

ILLUSTRATIONS

INTRODUCTION.

If the title " The Fifteen Decisive Battles of the World " be taken in its full meaning, to assert a certain philosophy of history, one might combat it by alleging the decisive character of fifteen events of a different kind, for example, " The Fifteen Decisive Love-Affairs of the World." The second title has as much plausibility as the first. Did not Antony lose half a world for Cleopatra's voluptuous charms? Was not the Conqueror born of the chance meeting of Robert the Devil and a bare-foot girl? In how far was the poet Gray right in saying that the Reformation in England was due to " the gospel light that dawned in Boleyn's eyes "?

Perhaps the cleanest, and surely the most momentous, of historic love-affairs was that of Friar Martin and Sister Catharine, who, convinced that their vows of celibacy were wrong and void, married each other on June 13, 1525. The act, symbolizing and crowning the whole revolt from Rome, created an immense sensation throughout Europe. The rage of the Catholics at " the monk Priapus and the nun Venus " was, for the most part, expressed in language not fit to be repeated. Henry VIII, from the vantage-ground of his own superior domestic life, had the bridal couple put into a scurillous comedy, and his chancellor, Sir Thomas More, could not miss the opportunity of mocking at " Friar Luther and Cate Callate, his nun, lusking together in lechery." Surely, said men, Antichrist must now come, — for was it not prophesied that he should be born of the union of a monk and a nun? Erasmus expressed the shrewd suspicion that Antichrist need not have waited so long to appear, and affected to take the thing lightly. Hitherto, said he, we have considered the Reformation a tragedy, but now, as it ends in a wedding, we know it to be a comedy. Even Luther's followers were not all pleased. Poor, timid Melanchthon shook his head over it in the most lugubrious way. Truly, as the bridegroom remarked of his marriage, " the angels laughed, and the devils wept thereat."

Undisturbed by the general storm, the newly married couple settled down to twenty years of quiet, domestic happiness. Their love for each other was of the deepest, best kind. Luther confessed in letters to friends, that, when he kissed his wife, he thanked God " for this best little creature of his."

INTRODUCTION

During the first year of marriage, "Katie," as her husband always called her, would sit by him at his work, trying to think up questions to ask.

But soon her leisure was taken up with the cares of a large house and family. Six children came to her in time, — Hans, a good, honest fellow; Elizabeth whose early death left her father "wonderfully sick at heart and almost womanish"; Magdalene, a lovely little girl who died in her fourteenth year; Martin, a rather sickly boy, for a time his father's "dearest treasure"; Paul, the brilliant member of the family; and Margaret.

After his marriage, as before, Luther continued to live in the large and handsome brick building which had once been the Augustinian cloister. The general exodus of its inmates, following the Reformer's proclamation of monastic emancipation, had left it nearly empty. At first assigned to him as a temporary residence, it was, in 1532, deeded by the government to him and his wife jointly. As professor in the university the Reformer received a sufficient salary, about the equivalent, in purchasing power, to that now paid to teachers in the larger institutions of learning. The great thrift of Frau Luther, and the bounty of princes, enabled her to accumulate a considerable property, notwithstanding her husband's unbounded liberality and hospitality.

For the great house was always full to the brim. Besides keeping a number of his own and Katie's poor relatives, the Reformer entertained many distinguished guests from abroad, and a constant quota of poor students. The latter paid for their board in services, usually clerical, but sometimes menial. The janitor, indeed, Wolfgang Sieberger, had come to Wittenberg as a student of theology, but, unable to keep up with the very modest requirements of the class-room, adapted himself to a humbler ministry.

Regarding the master with unlimited veneration, it was quite natural that these men should keep a record of all that he said, not only of his formal utterances in pulpit and lecture-room, but also of his lightest words at meals and by the evening fireside. The first to conceive this idea, according to his own account, was Conrad Cordatus, a grizzled Austrian, older than his host. Converted to Protestantism and ordained to the ministry, he was unfortunately able to keep neither his temper nor the various positions secured for him. The long intervals while he was out of work he spent at Wittenberg, and it was during one of these, in 1531, that, notwithstanding some qualms of delicacy, he began to write in a note-book all that he heard his host say at table. He was not on the best of terms with his hostess, and his importunity occasionally got him a snub from Luther himself.

His example was promptly followed by others. The first of these was Veit (Guy) Dietrich, a lad who acted as Luther's private secretary during the years 1529–1534, in which capacity he accompanied his master to Feste Coburg during the summer of 1530. While at Wittenberg he fell in love with Luther's niece and protégée, Magdalene Kaufmann. On Veit asking for her hand, her uncle replied: " I know that my niece would be well cared for by you, but I am not sure that you would be well cared for by her. She must be better brought up. If she does not behave better I will give her to a black smelter, and not cheat a pious, learned man with her." This refusal damped the ardor of the young people, each of whom shortly found consolation elsewhere. Dietrich took a number of private pupils, and it was his attempt to introduce them all into the Black Cloister (as the Luther house was called)

that led to a vigorous protest from Katie,
and his own subsequent withdrawal. As
pastor at Nuremberg for many years after,
he gave satisfaction.

A third reporter was John Schlaginhaufen,
a pale youth so obsessed with remorse for
his sins that he occasionally fell into fits,
from which he was recalled by the ghostly
advice and comfort of his revered master.
In later life he recovered sufficiently to fill
a small pastorate creditably.

Katie was not always pleased to see the
students get so much instruction gratis.
In advising her husband to charge them for
it, she noted, almost with jealousy, that
Anthony Lauterbach got the most and the
best. As his voluminous manuscripts testify,
this true-hearted young fellow did indeed
evince an almost superhuman diligence in
letting absolutely no gem of wisdom escape
him. Not content with what he heard himself, during two long visits in 1533 and again
from 1536 to 1539, he copied all the notes
he could collect from others, and spent a
considerable portion of his existence in
arranging and rearranging the separate sayings in topical order.

His friend Jerome Weller, who spent nine
years (1527–1536) of study at Wittenberg

as a guest of the Black Cloister, also took copious notes. Another reporter was Lewis Rabe, a refugee from the tyranny of Albert, Archbishop of Mainz. From one of Luther's letters we learn that he sat at table " like a maiden," apparently saying little but hearing much. Still another member of this devoted company was Nicholas Medler, one of the very smallest satellites revolving about and reflecting the rays of Germany's great luminary.

By the end of 1539 all the students just mentioned had left, but their places were speedily taken by others no whit less zealous. The first of these, both in time and in importance, was John Mathesius. For many years a schoolmaster, he never gave up the hope of becoming a minister, and at the age of thirty-six a lucky speculation in mines proved the providential means of fulfilling his pious wishes. From May to November, 1540, he was Luther's guest. When, at the latter end of his stay, he endeavored to use the Black Cloister as a boarding-school for his private pupils, the Reformer consented to receive as many as four of the boys, but, as the number grew, requested them to seek another refectory — more expensive, perhaps, if less inspiring. Mathesius, however,

kept his records, and published some of
them later in his biography of the master
(1566). His manuscript as a whole, however, had to wait three hundred and fifty
years to see the light.

With Mathesius were a few other students
of whom little need be said. There was
George Plato of Hamburg, who lodged as
well as boarded at the Black Cloister in
1540; there was Caspar Heydenreich a
little later (1541–3), and Jerome Besold
(1544) and John Stolz (1542–6). Nor are
these all the names that might be mentioned. So much the fashion did it become to
improve each shining hour at the master's
table, that many a transient guest has left
his own tiny sheaf of gleanings. It would
serve no purpose to enumerate them all,
but we must not omit to notice George Rörer,
a Wittenberg deacon, for twenty years the
chief secretary and literary factotum of the
Reformer. Though never a boarder at the
quondam friary, he was a frequent guest,
and has left a record of some conversations.

The last of the students to take notes,
and the first to publish them, was John
Aurifaber of Mansfeld, who came to the
Reformer as an amanuensis in 1545, and remained with him during the last year of his

life, being present at his death at Eisleben, on February 18, 1546. Later he took Lauterbach's large collection, added to it, and published it in 1566. Just five years later a man named Rebenstock turned Lauterbach's collection into Latin, and published it in that form.

It is not impossible to imagine what an evening with Luther must have been. The Black Cloister is still standing, and the living rooms, one flight up, to the front, are preserved as they were. One of them, handsomely wainscotted in dark wood, was used as the dining-room, apparently served by a small spiral staircase leading to the kitchen on the ground floor. Furnished with a long table, and low, comfortable chairs and benches, it was also ornamented with silver and crystal goblets, and with paintings by Lucas Cranach, including both portraits and allegorical pictures. In summer, flowers were not lacking; in winter, a large tile stove diffused a pleasant warmth.

As the day began at four or five, and as the principal meal was at ten A.M., supper was served about five, leaving a few hours for literary work or for conversation before bedtime at nine. Generous portions of pork, sausage, rye-bread and other plain food were washed down with copious draughts of home-brewed beer, or, on great occasions, with wine. Under the genial influence of the warmth, the company and the liquor, the Reformer, wearied by a day of hard toil, would unbend in a flow of conversation, employing a mixture of Latin and German. At the far end of the table the group of children surrounding Katie would not disturb him sitting at the head among his guests and students, some of whom were always straining over their notebooks, anxious lest the least word of the great man should fall into oblivion.

And what did he talk about? Literally, everything. Sometimes it was a personal reminiscence, perhaps of his far-off, unhappy boyhood at Mansfeld, or of his student-life at Erfurt, or of his spiritual agonies in the cloister, or of the journey to Rome and all he saw there — the pomp and glory, the unexampled corruption and wickedness of the capital of Christendom. Again he would tell how he attacked indulgences in 1517, or debated with Eck at Leipsic, or made the great stand at Worms, in which he "played a game with the pope that no king or emperor ever played." Or, coming to later years, he would inveigh against those "beasts," the peasants, who almost spoiled his work by their inopportune revolt in 1525. Or he would speak of his enemies, while his eyes flashed " with good, fresh wrath." How unbridled is his language! " I will curse a pater-noster against the papacy, that it get an epileptic fit "; " I will sing Psalm lxiv for a farewell to the papists and hope they will howl ' Amen ' to it." Nor was such language unpleasing to the men of that day, as it is to us. " My wrath is God's wrath," Luther once said, and Melanchthon added: " Yes, it is a heroic virtue! "

Nor were his anathemas confined to the papists. He once remarked that there " was a regular fraternity of skeptics in Germany," and the list of men he nominated for membership in this club was large. Conrad Mutian was an atheist because he taught that all religions were one; Erasmus was an atheist because he criticised the text of the New Testament; Carlstadt was an atheist because he denied the Real Presence in the sacrament; Campanus was worse than an atheist because he was a Unitarian. If Copernicus was not an atheist it was simply because he was nothing but a big fool for asserting that the earth went around the sun. So with many earnest and pious men. In that day tolerance was indeed rare; everybody was as bad in this respect as Luther, or at least as bad as he could be.

Often Luther talked of books, and very sound and trenchant opinions he often gave of them. History, particularly of the church, furnished him with much matter; the wickedness of the popes (especially Alexander VI) and the virtues of Huss and the martyrs were often on his tongue. Much he had to say of God, both of his wrath and of his mercy; much of his own doctrines and especially of faith, faith without works. The Bible, the translation and exegesis of which was his life-work, was also a constant theme.

But it is not only his weightier words that have come down to us. The students were as much without reserve as the master. Nothing was too sacred, nothing was too trivial for them. Luther's heart-rending grief at the death of his daughter, and Luther's idle jests and coarse stories are all repeated as if by dictograph. For, strange as it may seem to us, the pious man's conversations with his students contained many a free tale of the flesh, and many a word and phrase now banished from good society. In this he has at least the excuse of his time.

INTRODUCTION

" No great man," it has been well said,[1] " ever feared coarseness; little men cannot afford to be found ill-bred." The most unpleasant of Luther's indelicate sayings are those about his own wife. For these it is hard to find an excuse even in the practice of the time; he might have learned better from Erasmus.[2]

Far more to Luther's discredit than his occasional coarseness of speech were his harsh utterances concerning the German peasants, the class from which he himself sprang. The peasants were no doubt dull of comprehension, inappreciative of their blessings, and sometimes brutal, but they hardly deserved to be called " beasts " and " swine." The Reformer claimed that they had more to be thankful for than the nobles themselves, but surely his judgment on this point was sadly warped. And one must regret also his narrow intolerance of those who differed from him, even slightly, in religious matters. His relentless condemnation of sincere reformers like Zwingli, and his bitter

[1] *The Atheneum*, January 13, 1912, review of Aristophanes.

[2] "Multo minus decet maritos apud alios jactare formam conjugum suarum. Sed his quoque faciunt indecentius, qui quidquid in thalamo, quidquid in lecto cum uxore nugantur, depraedicant in conviviis et in colloquiis apud quoslibet. Si turpe est effere quod inter pocula dictum est, quanto turpius est ea non continere, quorum oportebat solum cubile torumque conscium esse?" "Lingua," *Erasmi opera*, 1703, iv, 686.

persecution of certain apparently harmless Anabaptists who came within his reach, grew out of the same medieval attitude of mind which made possible the horrors of the Inquisition and the religious wars.

On the other hand the reader of these verbatim reports of Luther's familiar talk cannot fail to be impressed with the man's abounding humor, which no doubt stood him in good stead in many a time of trial, as well as with the good sense with which he answered most of the questions that were put to him. Charming also are his love of children, his fondness for music, his liberality and disinterestedness, his hearty appreciation of life's blessings and his strong, simple faith in Christ. But how often and with what agony of soul he had to struggle with temptation! To him the devil and witches were real beings, assailing Christians in many ways and to be contended against constantly. At times he was almost overcome by despair. Evil influences seemed on the increase. The world seemed so incorrigible! But melancholy moods, occasioned, perhaps, by bodily illness, soon yielded to the spirit of hopefulness and courage, and to an enormous and self-sacrificing industry. It no doubt helped him also to be able to pour out his soul so freely as he did to his intimate companions.

Taken as a whole, there is in all literature no more charming or fascinating book than these intimate revelations of Luther's heart. All the autobiographies and " confessions " of men claiming to lay bare their souls, in reality reveal but a certain pose, generally conscious, but sometimes not. There is indeed Pepys, who wrote a diary in cypher with equal, though no greater, unreserve than that with which Luther talked. But what a difference in the men! On the one hand a little rogue and coxcomb, on the other a heart and brain of the first order of greatness. It is Froude who calls the table talk " one of the most brilliant books in the world," and " as full of matter as Shakespeare's plays." It is Mérimée who writes to his Unknown Lady: " The other night when I could hardly breathe I read Luther's table talk. I like the big man with all his prejudices and his hatred for the devil."

It is not remarkable that the book has enjoyed unbounded popularity. Besides countless reprints of the German, it has been translated into several other languages — twice into English. The first time was by

Captain Henry Bell, a soldier of fortune who served in various diplomatic and military positions abroad, chiefly in Brandenburg, during the years 1606-1618. He then held a sinecure office for some years, but in 1631, on the charge of forging German passports and other " foul frauds " was thrown into prison for about ten years. Here he employed his leisure in translating the table talk. The German copy he used, printed at Frankfort in 1574, may now be seen at Sidney Sussex College, Cambridge. He sent his manuscript first to Archbishop Laud, who kept it two years and returned it with a present of fifty pounds. He then sent it to the Commons with the purpose not only to secure sole license to print, but to get an order that the book should be put in every church in England, as had been done in the case of the Bible and of Erasmus' *Paraphrases*. The former request was granted, in an order of February 24, 1646-7; the latter was apparently referred to " an Assembly of divines " (Convocation?). These reverend gentlemen reported, May 3, 1647, that although the book contained many good things, yet there were also many passages contrary to truth, gravity and modesty, making it unfit for public use. The work finally appeared five years later under the title: *Martin Luther's Colloquia Mensalia, or his last Divine Discourses at his Table.* Notwithstanding the translator's assurance that he " had the High Dutch tongue very perfectly," his work is not scholarly, though the quaint old English is pleasant.

Another translation of the table talk was made in 1848 by William Hazlitt, son of the celebrated essayist. In his introduction and critical work he leans very heavily on the French version made by Gustave Brunet four years before, copying all the mistakes of this book, even to misprints in proper names. It is also probable that Bell's translation is made largely from the French. At any rate it is very inaccurate, though, in default of a better, and because of its easy style, it has been popular and has been often reprinted.

The aim of the present translation is not, however, so much to correct the faults of previous ones as to bring new and important material to the attention of the English-speaking public. Until the present generation practically all that was known of the table talk was the edition of Aurifaber, and as an editor this person treated his material with extreme freedom — suppressing, omitting, expanding, and altering, to suit his own pious, rather than scholarly, purposes. The publication of the original records in recent years has for the first time offered a really good text and has also brought to light much that was unknown to Aurifaber. The first of these new sources to be published was Lauterbach's "Diary for 1538," printed in 1872. Thirteen years afterwards Cordatus's notes were given to the public, and three years later those of Schlaginhaufen. The records of Mathesius, Rabe and Heydenreich, with some of Lauterbach's and Weller's, were published by Lösche in 1892, and, from a much better manuscript, with additional notes of Besold and Plato, by Kroker in 1903. The important manuscripts of Dietrich and Medler did not issue from the press until 1912. As there are no more sources of importance as yet unpublished, the moment seems propitious for using this vast amount of new material. So voluminous is it that a selection only is practicable, but, though comparatively small, the present chrestomathy, it is hoped, will present to the reader of English most of the new material of first importance and serve to represent fairly well the atmosphere of Luther's environment as well as the personal characteristics and opinions of the Reformer himself.

Finally the editors desire to express their obligation to Professors William L. Cowles and Clarence W. Eastman of Amherst College for aid in the interpretation of various passages, and to Dr. Winifred Smith of Vassar College for suggestions as to the arrangement of the material.

P. S.
H. P. G.

Introduction to the
Shepherd Classics Edition

Martin Luther was a giant, both intellectually and spiritually. He was also a warm human being. All of this becomes clear in *Table Talk*, published from the notes of students and friends, some of whom may not have understood fully or exactly what he was saying.

Everything Martin Luther said was eagerly devoured by the people of his time, caught up in the excitement of the freedom he proclaimed —the freedom of the sons and daughters of God, living their lives by faith in Jesus Christ under the law of perfect liberty.

One can imagine the conversations that gave rise to *Table Talk*. They probably occurred on those benches around the living room in Martin Luther's own home, where students gathered in the evening to enjoy the warmth of the porcelain stove that is still there. It was probably the only heated room in the house, and it became one of the warmest places in the whole University of Wittenberg. A winsome man full of the love of the Lord lived there, and a whole family grew up there to make this new parsonage a model of the Christian home for the next four centuries.

Because of the nature of the reporting, it cannot be said that *Table Talk* is the authoritative statement of Martin Luther's views. However, it is a source of great interest regarding this remarkable man whose faith in Christ made him the robust character he was.

In a world that is becoming cynical regarding the efforts of "image-makers," Luther stands out as a real man with real faith in God and real love toward other people. Instead of the lofty and vague goal of the brotherhood of man, Martin Luther held forth the love of God toward real people, and the love of real people toward others around them. Power for such love, he said, comes from the grace of God. It is certain and concrete. It is in Jesus Christ.

God loves people, and people can love God. All that love is born at the foot of Christ's cross. It is the love which the world needs and which the world has too little of. It is the secret of life today and tomorrow.

A superb translation of "Conversations with

Luther" by the great historian, Preserved Smith, and his associate, Herbert Percival Gallinger, gives to the world today some of the humanity of Martin Luther, together with a great insight into the origins of the Protestant Reformation gained from personal conversations around the table with such a courageous and warm-hearted character as Martin Luther.

Oswald C. J. Hoffman
St. Louis, Missouri
July 1979

CONVERSATIONS WITH LUTHER

1. LUTHER'S CHILDHOOD.

"One should not whip children too hard. My father once whipped me so severely that I fled from him and it was difficult for him to win me back again to himself. I would not willingly strike little Hans[1] much, for if I did he would be shy of me and hate me, than which no greater sorrow could happen to me. God acts in this way, for he says: 'I will chastize you, my children, (*i. e.*, by Satan or the world) but if you cry and come unto me I will take you and raise you up.' For God does not like us to hate him."

Then Luther said children should not be permitted to steal, but that mildness should be used if they only stole cherries or apples. "Those boyish pranks are not to be severely punished; it is time to punish when tehy begin on money, clothes or boxes. My parents were so strict that they made me cowardly. My mother beat me until the blood flowed, for the sake of a single nut. And by this strict discipline they finally forced me into the monastery, though they

[1] His own oldest son, born June 7, 1526. Luther speaks in 1532.

meant heartily well by it. They could not read dispositions and how to suit correction to them. The apple and the switch[1] should go hand in hand. It is a bad thing if children lose their spirit on account of parents and teachers. There have been many bungling masters who have hurt splendid talents by nagging. Ah, what a time we had with the *lupus*[2] on Fridays and Donatus[3] on Thursdays! They asked strictly of each one to parse ' legeris, legere, legitur, lecti mei ars.' These questions were like a trial for murder. Good method in teaching should note differences of character in pupils."

When someone asked Luther how he would interpret the text: " Provoke not your children to wrath,"[4] he replied: " Have you read your Terence? ' According to the common practice of fathers, I daily nagged him etc.'[5] This sentence means that chil-

[1] *I. e.*, reward and punishment.

[2] The *lupus*, or wolf, was the monitor who punished the boys for not speaking Latin.

[3] Donatus, on the Parts of Speech, was the common Latin text-book.

[4] Ephesians vi, 4.

[5] The reference is to the comedy of Terence, *Heauton-timorumenos* (The Self-tormentor), Act 1, line 49. Menedemus, who is doing penance for having driven his only son from home by harsh treatment, regrets that instead of using kindness he resorted to force, " according to the common practice of fathers."

dren should be so educated that they are not made timid. If one is a Demea,[1] then he makes children either faint-hearted or desperate; accordingly they do what otherwise they would no doubt leave undone. Children ought to be flogged, but also they should be given food and drink, that they may see that we should like to have them virtuous. Thus Solomon says: ' Chasten thy son, but turn not thy mind to his destruction! '[2] One ought to educate a child, where there is hope of success; but if one sees that there is no hope, and that he can learn nothing, one ought not to whip him to death on that account, but train him for something else. Some teachers are as cruel as hangmen. For instance I was once whipped fifteen times before noon, for no fault of mine, for I was expected to decline and conjugate what I had not yet learned. Anthony Tucher of Nuremberg used to say: ' Praise and punishment both have a place in ruling.' Hence one should be kind and friendly to little people and none the less continue the whipping."

Luther often spoke at length about witchcraft, about pressure at the heart and night-

[1] See Terence's play, *Adelphi* (The Brothers). Demea, one of the brothers, is a harsh and violent father.

[2] Proverbs xix, 18.

mare,[1] and how his mother was troubled by a neighbor who was a witch, to whom she was obliged to be very respectful and conciliating, for otherwise the woman plagued her children and made them cry themselves to death. A certain preacher chided her in a manner; he was then poisoned and died, for no medicine could cure him, for she took earth from his footprints, bewitched it and threw it into the water, and without this earth he could not recover. Luther was then asked whether such things could happen to pious people. "Yes," said he, "our minds are subject to falsehoods just as our bodies are to murders. I think that my illnesses are not natural but are mere bewitchments. But God will free his elect from these evils."

[1] "Alpdrucken" and "Alptraum," both caused, in superstitious belief, by an incubus.

2. AT ERFURT UNIVERSITY, 1501-1505, AND THE ERFURT FRIARY, 1505–1508, 1509–1511.

When Luther wished to return home and was on the road, by chance he struck his sword with his leg and cut an artery. He was then alone in a field with one companion, about as far from Erfurt as Eutzsch is from Wittenberg (half a mile).[1] Thereupon the blood flowed alarmingly and could not be checked. When he tried to stop it with his finger, the leg swelled to an amazing size. At length a surgeon was called from the town, who cured the wound. When he was in danger of death, he said: "O Mary, help!" ("Had I died then," said he, "I should have died calling on Mary.") Again in bed during the night the wound broke open, and as his strength failed he again called on Mary. It was the Tuesday after Easter.[2]

[1] The German mile varied in different provinces; its length was usually four or five times that of an English mile.

[2] The year of this incident is uncertain, although the editors of the Weimar edition of the Table Talk conjecture that it occurred in 1503. Apparently Luther was at the time a student of the University of Erfurt and was on his way home to Mansfeld. The account here given is from the notes of Veit Dietrich.

Once when Luther was a young man, he happened upon a copy of the Bible,[1] where he read by chance the story of the mother of Samuel in the book of Kings; the volume pleased him exceedingly, and he thought he would be happy if he could ever possess one. A little later he bought a book of homilies[2]; this pleased him greatly, for it contained more of the gospels than was usually learned during a year.

When he entered the monastery he left behind him all his books. He had secured a little before the *Corpus Juris* and I know not what other books. These he handed over to the library. He took none into the monastery with him except Plautus and Vergil. There the monks gave him a Bible bound in red leather. With this he made himself so familiar, that he knew the contents of every page, and whenever any sentence was presented to him, he knew at once where it was written. " If I had retained this knowledge," he said, " I should have been a wonderfully good biblical con-

[1] This was during his student days at Erfurt. See Smith, *Martin Luther*, p. 6. On another occasion Luther said that when he was twenty he had not yet seen a Bible (see below, p. 10); if therefore his memory did not fail him, the incident here referred to must have occurred after 1503.

[2] "Postil," a book containing expositions of those portions of Scripture appointed to be read at divine service.

cordance," and he added: "No study then attracted me but sacred literature. I found physics extremely tedious, and my soul would burn to get back to the Bible. I used the ordinary gloss.[1] Lyra[2] I despised, although afterwards I came to see that he was valuable for history. I read the Bible, however, with diligence; a single important sentence would occupy my thoughts for a whole day, and in the major prophets there were sentences which clung to me (though I could not comprehend them), and which I remember yet, as that in Ezekiel: 'For I have no pleasure in the death of him that dieth, saith the Lord God; wherefore turn yourselves and live ye.'"[3]

"I, Martin Luther, entered the monastery against the will of my father and left it to his joy. For he understood the rascality of monks. On the day on which I said my first mass,[4] he said to me: 'Son, do you not know that you should honor your father? Suppose that it was only a ghost that you saw.'[5]

[1] The "Glosa Ordinaria," a popular medieval commentary.
[2] Nicholas de Lyra was the author of an extensive commentary on the Bible, much used in the Middle Ages.
[3] Ezek. xviii, 32.
[4] May 2, 1507; cf. Smith, op. cit., p. 10.
[5] This refers to Luther's belief that he had been warned to enter the monastery by a heavenly vision, connected with a thunderstorm. *American Journal of Psychology*, xxiv, 369 (1913).

And when I began to say mass according to the rule, I was so frightened that I would have fled had I not been admonished by the prior. When I came to the words: ' Thee, most merciful Father,' the thought that I had to speak to God without a mediator made me want to flee like Judas before the world. For who can bear the majesty of God without Christ as mediator? As a monk I experienced all those horrors; I had to experience them before I could fight them."

" After the pope by force and fraud had seized all power and authority, so that neither king nor emperor could humble him, then it had to be that the son of perdition should be revealed by the power of the Word. I came to the task unawares. For twenty years ago I should never have believed that even if another had taught as I did, I should have condemned the pope, and, as it were, burned him. But God is the cause of such wondrous works. True, when I was a young master at Erfurt,[1] (at which time I was much subject to melancholy), I applied myself much to reading the Bible, and from its text alone saw the many errors of the papacy. But then, in the Erfurt library[2]

[1] 1505.
[2] The library of the Augustinian convent at Erfurt is still shown. The building is now used as an orphan asylum.

[8]

I would think: 'Behold how great is the authority of the church and of the pope. Are you alone wise? You also may err.' I gave place to these thoughts and was thereby hindered in reading the Bible. Afterwards, when I saw the crass abuse of indulgences, I disputed against it. When they would not yield an inch I proceeded, although I alone labored for three years[1] in the cause I had taken up, and despaired of it. Certain brothers wrote exhorting me to constancy, and one excellent man, personally unknown to me, came to me in this very spot[2] praying with tears that I should proceed against the papacy, because I would thereby bring great advantage to the church. Staupitz encouraged me much. When he was in Rome in 1511[3] he heard the prophecy publicly proclaimed: An Eremite[4] shall arise and spoil the papacy. A certain Franciscan at Rome had seen this in a vision. But God guided the matter wonderfully and drove me on unwittingly in the cause. He alone has brought it so far that between the pope and

[1] 1517-20.

[2] *I.e.* in the Augustinian cloister at Wittenberg, later the Luther house.

[3] Staupitz was in Italy in 1510; nothing else is known of his being there in 1511, but it is possible. H. Böhmer, *Luthers Romfahrt*, 1914, p. 29.

[4] The Augustinians were called Eremites, or hermits.

us there can be no toleration. For it does not suit the pope to yield in one little error, and contrariwise it is not lawful for us to give in to him in the smallest article. Wherefore may God help us, should man fail us. As long as I can I will help God to fight the pope. And if those ranters,[1] Münzer, Carlstadt and the Anabaptists had not interfered, all would have gone excellently. For when I alone had borne the brunt of the battle they wished to run off with the prize. They fished with my nets, but by their plan to destroy the pope they really helped him.

" Thirty years ago no one read the Bible;[2] it was unknown to all. The prophets were not mentioned nor could they be understood. When I was twenty years old I had not yet seen a Bible. I thought there was neither gospel nor epistle except what was contained in the Sunday lessons. At length I found a Bible in the library, and when I entered the monastery I began to read it, to reread it and to read it again. Staupitz was much astonished. In those days of

---

[1] On them *cf.* Smith, *op. cit.*, chap. xiii.

[2] Luther speaks on February 22, 1538. This is a gross exaggeration; the Bible was apparently much studied at the opening of the sixteenth century, but the enormous popularity of Luther's translation made him feel that it was comparatively little known previously.

darkness the pope ruled with superstition and guile, whose angelic splendor I should never have dared to attack had not St. Paul in the clearest words showed the future blindness of the papacy and had not Christ, Majesty itself, hurled down the pope with such fulminations as: 'In vain do they worship me, teaching for doctrines the commandments of men.'[1] . . . When a certain cardinal at Rome took counsel against me early in my career, a court fool is reported to have said: ' My Lord, follow my advice and first depose Paul from the company of the apostles; he troubles us more than the others.' "

" Formerly when I was a monk they despised the Bible. No one understood the Psaltery. They believed the Epistle to the Romans had some disputes about matters of Paul's time, and was of no use for our age. Scotus, Aquinas and Aristotle were to be read. But I loved the Bible. When I began to apply myself to the Psalms I first tried to get the general argument and then to understand the meaning of every word. My Katie[2] now understands the Psalms better than all the papists. A doctor once

[1] Matthew xv, 9.
[2] *I.e.*, his wife. Luther is speaking in 1540. The Psalms had always been dear to him.

said: 'The Psaltery is the book for the highest and holiest theologians.'"

" I wandered long and knew not where I was. I felt a need but knew not what it was until I came to the place in Romans[1] 'The just shall live by faith.' That helped me. There I saw of what justice Paul speaks. In the text 'justice' came first. So I put together the abstract and the concrete, and came to know my trouble and distinguish between the justice of the law and that of the gospel. Before that nothing helped me, for I made no distinction between the law and the gospel. I thought them all one, and said Christ differed from Moses only in degree and in time, but when I saw that the law was one thing and the gospel another I broke through my difficulties."

Luther told a story of what had happened to him while a young monk at Erfurt. He went to preach[2] in a certain village and when

[1] Romans, i, 17. This experience of Luther, which stands at the head of his career, and which he more fully describes elsewhere, 1545 (*Opera latina varii argumenti*, i, 15ff) has been placed in different years. It probably occurred in 1515; see "Luther's development of the doctrine of Justification by Faith," *Harvard Theological Review*, vi, 240 (1913).

[2] "terminatum." Explained by referring to Du Cange: *Glossarium mediae et infimæ latinæ:* Terminarii apud Ordines Mendicantes dicuntur qui habendis per agros cuique conventui addictos concionibus destinantur.

he was ready to say mass the village priest[1]
began to sing the *Kyrie eleison* and the
Paternoster to the accompaniment of a lute.
" So I had to say mass though I could hardly
keep from laughing. For I was not used to
such an organ and had to sing my *Gloria in
excelsis* to his *Kyrie*."

" When I was a monk I did not want to
omit any of the prescribed prayers, and
when I was pressed by lecturing and writing
I often could not say the appointed hours for
a whole week, or sometimes for two or three
weeks. Then I would take two or three days
off, and would eat and drink nothing until
I had said all the prayers omitted. That
made my head so crazy that for hours together I never closed my eyes, and became
deathly sick and went out of my senses.
And when I got better and tried to read,
suddenly my head would go bad again.
Thus God drew me as it were by
force from that rack of prayer. So you
see how much I was captive to the tra-
ditions of men. Wherefore I easily forgive
those who find difficulty in assenting to my
doctrine."

" At Erfurt one time I said to Dr. Staupitz:
' My dear doctor, our Lord God treats people

[1] "custos." See Du Cange.

[13]

too abominably! Who can serve him when he strikes people down right and left, as he does many of our adversaries?' Dr. Staupitz replied: 'Learn, I beg of you, to look at God differently. If he did not do this, how could he quell the obstinate? God is fighting in a good cause, that he may save us, who otherwise would be oppressed.' His treatment of our adversaries made clear to me at Coburg[1] the meaning of those words in the decalogue: 'I am a jealous God.' For the punishment meted out to them is not so cruel as our defence is necessary. Thus they say that Zwingli has perished, whose error, had it prevailed, would have destroyed us along with our church. It is a judgment of God. The Swiss have always been a proud people. The others, the papists, our Lord God will also find. The Zwinglians called God 'a God made bread,'[2] but now it will come to pass that he will be an iron God to them. Œcolampadius called the Lord's Supper [as celebrated by the

[1] Luther is speaking in 1531. In the preceding year he spent six months at Coburg, during the deliberations of the Diet of Augsburg.

[2] "Impanatum Deum." An allusion to the sacramentarian controversy. Luther insisted on the real presence of Christ's body in the bread of the eucharist; Zwingli said then that his God was not "incarnate" or "made flesh," but "impanate" or "made bread."

Lutherans] the feast of Thyestes,[1] flesh-eating, blood-drinking, etc. We now say to them, ' Here you have what you have sought. God once said that he would not hold him guiltless who took his name in vain.' It was exceedingly blasphemous to call God ' made bread ' and us flesh-eaters, blood-drinkers and God-devourers. The same thing will happen to our papists, who have burdened themselves with the blood of the righteous, and God grant that they become like a withered tree, which in the spring puts forth no shoots. They say themselves that they intend to suppress our teaching or lose all. Amen. Let it be as they desire! How can our Lord God better requite them than to give them what they wish? "

---

[1] According to the story Thyestes was invited to a banquet at which was served up to him the flesh of his own children.

3. THE JOURNEY TO ROME, DECEMBER 1510.

" At Rome there is a temple [the Pantheon], which I saw, with a round hole in the roof, and a high vault supported by marble pillars which three of us could hardly reach around. On the vault above are painted all the gods, Jupiter, Neptune, Mars and Venus as they were called. These gods conspired to drive the world mad, but Jesus Christ came and prevented them and swept them away. Then came the popes to strive against him, but who knows how long they will stand? "

" If there is a hell, Rome stands on it. I believe that Peter was at Rome, even if it cannot be proved from Scripture. Paul preached throughout the whole of Asia Minor and the Turkish country."

" The pope and his followers have perished by trusting to force, for if they had used moderation, zounds![1] what might they not have obtained? But the papacy deserved to perish, which they themselves confessed when I was at Rome. The papal court was

[1] The expletive used by Luther is *potz tausent fa, mi, re,* for which there is hardly an equivalent in English. See Grimm's *Worterbuch,* 6, a, 83.

then called the fountain of justice, but I learned that it was a harlot. Campeggio[1] said at Augsburg: ' Cajetan has destroyed this cause by attempting to use force in a matter that called for wise counsel and strategy.' "

Mentioning the city of Rome, Luther said: " Since now the Lord God has got me into this dreadful, hateful business, I would not have missed seeing and hearing what I did at Rome for a hundred thousand florins. I had to guard myself constantly lest I should commit some offence against God; but what we see, we relate. For Bembo,[2] a very learned man, said, after he had carefully considered the matter, that Rome was the cess-pool of humanity and of the whole world. And someone has written:

' Who seeks to live a holy life, from Rome
    must take his flight,
For everything is there allowed, except to
    be upright.'

Before the time of the Reformation, there were, quite frequently, men who scourged Rome's wickedness in the city itself; there

[1] Cardinal Campeggio was present at the Diet of Augsburg in 1530 as papal legate.

[2] A distinguished humanist, the Latin secretary of Leo X.

was one Louis, a Franciscan, and Giles of Viterbo, an Augustinian, and two other preachers, who, when they had severely censured the morals of the papacy, were found one morning with their tongues cut out. The pope's name is: ' Touch me not! ' " And then he related the story of a certain Jew, who, being about to accept the Christian faith, confessed to a priest that he intended to visit Rome first and inspect the head of Christendom before he was baptized. The priest sought earnestly to dissuade him from this plan, fearing lest, having seen the scandalous conditions at Rome, his opinion of Christianity would change, but the Jew, having journeyed thither, and having seen the many horrible things there, returned to the priest and consented to be baptized, saying: " Now I will gladly accept the God of the Christians, for he is so patient; if he can suffer such knavery as exists at Rome, he can easily bear all the sins of the world. For our God is pretty angry, and has tortured us, his own people, in various ways."[1]

" Rome as I, Luther, saw it, is a whole mile[2] square, being as wide as from here to Pollersberg. So far as one can judge, it

---

[1] This story is the second in Boccaccio's Decameron.
[2] A German mile, about four and a half English miles.

covers the whole plain." And then he read from histories the number of the Roman citizens: twenty years before the birth of Christ, 5,100,000 citizens; not long after that the number of Roman citizens was 6,900,000. Then Amsdorf[1] said that the city still commanded 500,000 men.[2] Erfurt has 18,000 houses, Venice 300,000. Nuremberg is scarcely half the size of Erfurt.

" Great is the power of the devil, and he is able to bewitch our eyes and minds, as he has done with the tunic[3] of Christ, and the image[4] of Christ which the Elector has, and the nun who put the cowdung on her head and imagined that she wore a crown.[5] Anna Lamenit, known as the Ursula of Augsburg, was not deceived herself, but she deceived others. I met her at Augsburg,[6] and asked whether she was willing to die, but she replied: ' Faith, no! How it goes there I do not know; but how it goes here, that I know.' "

[1] Nicholas von Amsdorf, Luther's most devoted follower.

[2] An absurd exaggeration. According to Gregorovius the population of Rome in 1527 before the city was sacked was 85,000, after the sack, 32,000. *Rome in the Middle Ages*, VIII, 556 *note*, 646.

[3] Luther refers to the seamless coats of Christ exhibited at various places.

[4] This had movable hands. See below, p. 82f.

[5] See *Luthers Werke*, Weimar Ed. I, 409.

[6] He saw the maid, who pretended that she ate nothing, in 1511 on his way back from Rome.

4. TEACHING AT WITTENBERG, 1508-9, AND 1511-46.

Someone said: " It is a wonder that such a university has arisen at Wittenberg among these Vandals." Luther answered: " God said to himself: ' I must raise up a university where I can make a preacher or two, for all the rest have failed.'

" Formerly there was enough money and sufficient salaries, for there were many students. Now there are many splendid minds, but the students are almost forced to beg. Here we sit at Wittenberg in a carrion land. For, according to Dr. Pollich,[1] Wittenberg is at the end of civilization. If we went a little further we should be in the midst of barbarism."

" It is too much for a human being to believe that God is gracious to him; the human mind cannot grasp it. How was it in my case? I shrank back once in terror from the sacrament, which Dr. Staupitz carried at Eisleben in the Corpus Christi procession.[2] On this occasion I walked with

[1] Martin Pollich of Mellerstadt, first rector of the University of Wittenberg, founded in 1502.

[2] Probably in 1515.

THE LIVING-ROOM of Luther's house at Wittenberg, furnished as it was in his day. Here most of the table-talk originated.

the rest and had on the dress of a priest.
Afterwards I confessed to Dr. Staupitz, and
he said to me: ' You have not the right idea
of Christ.' His words consoled me greatly.
Such is our nature that although Christ
offers himself to us with the remission of our
sins, yet we flee from his face, just as I once
fled in my boyhood days, when we were
singing for sausages.[1] At that time a towns-
man cried out, in fun: ' What are you doing,
you young scamps? The devil take you!'
At the same time he ran towards us with
two sausages. I and my companion took
to our heels, fleeing the gift which was being
offered us. We act in exactly the same way
toward God; he gave us Christ and all sorts
of gifts, and yet we flee him and think of
him as our judge."

Luther said concerning the university at
Wittenberg: " I warned Dr. Brück[2]: ' Whoever after my death disdains the authority of
this university, — if indeed church and university last so long; for at Antioch, Constantinople and at Rome also there were

[1] An incident of his school days at Eisenach, where he was
"obliged to help himself after the manner of poor scholars,
who, as he tells us, went about from door to door collecting
small gifts or doles by singing hymns." Koestlin, *Life of
Luther*, p. 14.

[2] Gregory Brück, often called Pontanus (1483 or 1486–
1557), at this time chancellor of Electoral Saxony.

excellent academies and yet they perished —
he is a heretic and a perverse man; for God
has revealed in this university his Word,
and today[1] this university and city may be
compared with all others both as to doctrine
and as to life, although we are not wholly
without fault in respect to the latter.'

"Whoever today are the greatest agree
with us, as Amsdorf,[2] Brenz[3] and Rhegius;[4]
they seek our friendship and correspond with
us. But whoever flee from us and secretly
scoff at us have abandoned the faith as
Jeckel and Grickel,[5] and Zwingli, too, who
have learned everything alone and nothing
from us. Who knew anything twenty-five
years ago? Who stood by me twenty-one
years ago,[6] when, against my will and knowledge, God led me into this game? Ah, vainglory [7] brings misfortune!"

[1] 1540.

[2] Nicholas von Amsdorf (1483–1565), professor at Wittenberg.

[3] John Brenz (1499–1570) a prominent reformer at Swabian
Halle. Life by G. Bayer, 1899.

[4] Urban Rieger (Regius or Rhegius, 1489–1541), also a
prominent reformer, at this time at Zell in Brunswick-Lüne-
burg.

[5] "Jeckel and Grickel," nicknames for James Schenk and
John Agricola, charged with antinomianism and expelled from
Saxony. Cf. Smith, op. cit., 282–5.

[6] Luther is speaking in August, 1540.

[7] Κενοδοξία, Philippians, ii, 3.

" The poorest youths are the most studious, for Christ, himself poor, wishes to build up his poor kingdom through poor men. The rich young gentlemen, loaded down with purse and possessions, do not study."

5. THE THESES ON INDULGENCES, 1517.

"I like Fleck.[1] He is a man full of comfort and his words are consolatory. He wrote me a letter, a splendid one, immediately after I had published my Theses. I would give ten gulden to have it now. Its purport was about as follows: 'Venerable Doctor, proceed! Press forward! These papal abuses always displeased me too, etc.' The monks were also angry at him, for he said to those at Steinlausig: '*There* is a man who will do something.' He never said a mass, which was a good sign."

Fleck was Prior of the Franciscans at Steinlausig.

6. THE INTERVIEW WITH CARDINAL CAJETAN AT AUGSBURG, OCTOBER, 1518.

"The cardinal at Augsburg said of me: 'That brother has deep eyes and so must have strange fancies in his head.'[1]

"I went to Augsburg when first cited, with a safe-conduct from the elector, who recommended me to the care of the citizens of Augsburg, begging that they should take care of me and not let me converse with the Italians nor trust in them. For I knew not how serious the matter was. I was at Augsburg three days without a safe-conduct from the emperor. In the meantime an Italian[2] came to summon me to the cardinal and to urge me to recant. He said: 'Only utter this one word, *revoco*, then the cardinal will commend you to the pope and you will return with glory to your elector.' After three days had elapsed the bishop of Trent in the name of the emperor showed my safe-conduct to the cardinal. Then I went to

---

[1] Myconius, *Historia Reformationis*, p. 30, also tells this story. The same remark has been attributed to Dr. Martin Pollich, the rector of Wittenberg. *Cf.* Köstlin-Kawerau, i, 87.

[2] Urban de Serralonga. *Cf.* Smith, *op. cit.*, 48f.

him as a suppliant, first throwing myself on my knees, then bowing to the earth and then falling flat on my face, and only rising humbly after the cardinal had thrice asked me to do so. This greatly pleased him, for it gave him hope of victory. But on the second day after I refused to recant, he said: ' What do you think the pope cares for Germany? Do you suppose the princes will defend you by arms?' — ' No' — ' Then where will you live?' — ' Under heaven.' Such was the miserable insolence of the pope. It is more bitter than death to him to have his dignity and majesty despised, but now he can't help it. At that time the pope humbled himself in a way by writing to the elector, or rather to Spalatin and Pfeffinger,[1] asking that they should hand me over and execute his mandate. He also wrote to the elector:[2] ' Although you are personally unknown to me, yet I saw your father Ernest at Rome, a most obedient son of the church, and a devout professor of religion. I hope your Highness will follow his example.' But the elector knew this unwonted humility of the pope was due to his bad conscience

[1] To both on October 24, 1518. P. Smith, *Luther's Correspondence*, i, 127.

[2] August 23, 1518. *Luther's Correspondence*, i. 105.

because he feared the power of Scripture. For my *Resolutions*[1] had circulated through almost the whole of Europe in a few days. So the elector was encouraged not to follow their commands but to submit to the judgment of Scripture. Had the cardinal at Augsburg acted more moderately and received me as a suppliant, things would never have gone so far. For up to that time I knew but little of the errors of the pope. Had he kept quiet I should have done the same. For it was the Roman custom when an obscure and intricate question came up for the pope to say: ' We reserve this to ourselves by virtue of our pontifical authority,' and thus he would quash it. Then both sides are forced to keep silence. I believe the pope would give three cardinals to have the matter in the same condition now as it was in then."

" You know not under what shadows we were in papal times. Gerson[2] was the best doctor, for he began the revolt, although unconscious of his trend. Nevertheless he raised the question whether the papal power should be obeyed in all things, and answered

[1] A work written in defence of the *Theses*, 1518. Smith, *Luther*, p. 44.
[2] The French cardinal distinguished at the Council of Constance. He lived from 1363 to 1429.

that it was not a mortal sin to disobey unless it were done contumaciously. He dared not drive the wedge home. Yet he comforted the people who called him the consoling teacher. He was condemned for it. The cardinal at Augsburg called me a Gersonist because I appealed from the pope to a council."[1]

[1] Text: "the Council of Constance," a mistake of the note-taker.

7. LUTHER'S RETURN FROM AUGSBURG, 1518.

When Luther had gone to Augsburg to meet Cajetan and had refused to recant, he was deserted by all human defenders, by the emperor, by the pope, by the cardinal legate, by his own prince, Frederic, Elector of Saxony, by his monastic order and by his most intimate friend Staupitz. Prince Frederic did not welcome him back from Augsburg, nor had he persuaded him to go there. Somewhat discouraged by this desertion, he took counsel with himself as to where he would go. In Germany there was no hope. In France it was not safe on account of the threats of the pope. Being therefore in the greatest perplexity, he returned to Saxony. On the first day he journeyed from Augsburg to Monheim. He had a hard trotting nag, no long trousers but only knee breeches; neither knife nor gun, nor spurs, yet thus he made the journey all the way to Wittenberg. When he came thither Charles von Miltitz, a nobleman from the papal court, was there. The latter had seventy letters from the pope addressed to the princes and the bishops to the effect that they should seize

Luther and send him to the pope at Rome. Prince Frederic, fearing lest he might be compelled by the authority of the pope to seize him, indicated to him that he should betake himself to some other place where he might safely lie concealed. He was forced to obey the prince. And so he invited his friends to take a meal with him that he might bid them good-bye, though he was uncertain as to where he was going. As they were about to sit down letters arrived from Spalatin[1] indicating that the prince was amazed that he had not yet gone, and that he should therefore hasten his departure. He was greatly affected by this message, thinking that he had been abandoned by all, but a little later becoming again hopeful, he said: " Father and mother forsook me, but the Lord took me up."[2] Not long afterwards, while they were still at table, other letters arrived with a message from Spalatin to the effect that if he had not yet gone he should remain, for Miltitz had proposed to the prince that the affair could be settled by a colloquy or debate. The prince giving heed to a more just opinion, kept the doctor, who has remained at Wittenberg even to the present day, July 30, 1535.

[1] Spalatin was the prince's private secretary.
[2] Psalm xxvii, 10.

8. CHARLES VON MILTITZ FAILS TO ARREST THE HERETIC. 1519.

Charles von Miltitz is known from the letter[1] of Luther to Leo X. The pope sent him to the Elector of Saxony with the golden papal rose, which was then a great gift and a singular mark of the pope's favor and which it was the custom to send with peculiar solemnity. Now the reason for this gift was this, that Prince Frederic might feel grateful to the pope and send him Luther as a captive in charge of Charles von Miltitz. For this purpose the pope had given Charles seventy apostolic letters, as they are called, in order that he might be permitted to journey in safety through the various cities with the captive Luther. These are not false things that I[2] write, for Luther said that he had heard them from Charles himself at Altenburg. And Charles certainly came to Germany with great hope of accomplishing his mission, but in this he was greatly mistaken. For he himself said that in the more

[1] Of March 3, 1519. De Wette, *Luthers Briefe*, No. cxxiv. This letter was never sent. *Cf.* P. Smith, *Luther's Correspondence*, vol. i, p. 166.
[2] Veit Dietrich makes these notes in 1532.

important cities of Germany he had made mention of Luther in various places and that all were so stirred up over the new fame of his doctrine that even though he had an army of thirty thousand Swiss soldiers, he would despair of bringing Luther all the way through Germany to Rome.

9. THE DIET OF WORMS, APRIL, 1521.

"I will kill Cochlaeus by silence only.[1] He is a little fool with his arguments and his dogmas; I will let him stick in them and not answer him. Was I not heard at Augsburg? Did I not appear at Worms even after they had violated my safe-conduct?[2] For I was cited by the emperor's herald on the second day of that painful week, but I was condemned on the fourth day, and my books were burned before I came to Erfurt and my condemnation was affixed to the gates of the city and in other public places. As I was on the journey to Worms the herald asked me if I really expected to appear there. I, though trembling, answered: 'I will come if all the devils are there.' When I was near, Bucer came to meet me, instigated by the emperor's confessor [Glapion] to warn me not to enter Worms unless I wished to be burned, and to advise me to withdraw

[1] Luther is speaking in September, 1532; for the moment he is thinking of a book written against him by John Dobneck, usually called Cochlaeus.

[2] Luther considered the mandate of Charles V commanding his books to be delivered to the magistrates a violation of the implied agreement that he should not be condemned until he had been heard.

to the protection of Francis von Sickingen. But I went on, and when I had arrived was entertained by the elector's councillors.

"None of the princes came to meet me but the nobility made much of me. Some of them submitted [to the emperor] four hundred articles against the clergy and proved them by my preaching. The Catholics were more frightened than I was; they dreaded a rising, for the pope had stirred the people up and had written that my safe-conduct should not be respected. To this request the princes were unwilling to accede. When summoned I came into the assembly of the princes and the emperor. First I was asked if the books were mine; I replied: 'I think so.' Dr. Jerome Schurff said: 'Let the titles be read.' Asked, in the second place, if I would recant I made a distinction. I said I could not revoke doctrinal statements, for they were the Word of God, but if my books contained intolerable invective I made no great matter of it and would let it be pointed out to me. A day and a night were given me to consider.[1] Then the bishops treated with me about recanting. I said to them: 'God's Word is God's Word, which

---

[1] Apparently something has been omitted here, describing Luther's second appearance at the Diet, April 18. *Cf.* Smith, *Luther*, 113ff.

I cannot recant. In the rest I will gladly obey.' Margrave Joachim of Brandenburg said that I should leave it to the emperor and asked if they were not also Christians? I answered: 'Let the Scripture be kept safe; I cannot give up what is not mine.' The committee of bishops urged that I ought to trust their judgment as to what was right. I answered: 'I do not trust you enough to believe that you would decide for me against yourselves, since you have already condemned me while I was coming.' . . . Then Cochlaeus came to me and said if I would waive my safe-conduct he would dispute with me. Schurff said: 'That would be unfair. Who would be so foolish?' But I would have done it in my simplicity. . . . After that Vehus, chaplain of the Margrave of Baden, invited me to recant, making a splendid oration, and saying that I owed much to brotherly love, much to obedience to the emperor, and much to the duty of avoiding scandal. I answered: 'True, but I owe more to Christ.' Then Dr. Eck, chancellor of Trier, said: 'Luther, though disobedient to the emperor you are allowed to go in peace. Do not preach on the road, and look out for yourself after the expiration of your safe-conduct.' I answered: 'As the Lord pleased it has come to pass. You also must look out for yourself.' Thus I won great glory at Worms and they wished the beer back in the bottles. As I supported my position from the Bible, Duke George always said: ' Then, gentlemen, my subjects must not be allowed to have it.' But I knew nothing of their wiles. The Elector Frederic once said: ' I did not think they would act so.' Then the Edict went out against all Lutherans, which, however, the Catholics wished to recall immediately. Thus it went with me at Worms where the Holy Spirit alone supported me."

" I could not easily tell with what wonderful schemes and tricks they sought to prevent my going to Worms and appearing before the emperor, in order that they might calumniate me by saying that I had fled the light. First they condemned me in a public warrant,[1] burning my books and affixing my condemnation to the doors throughout Germany. This they did by the advice of the Archbishop of Mainz who was then all powerful with the emperor. They wished to send Glapion, the emperor's confessor, to

[1] Shortly before Luther's appearance at Worms Charles V issued a mandate ordering his books to be delivered up and burned.

LUTHER'S ROOM at the Wartburg, where he lived from May 1521 to February 1522. The diamond-shaped hole in the wall has been cut by visitors. On it was originally a dark stain, said to have been caused by Luther throwing his inkstand at the devil.

Francis von Sickingen at Ebernburg; thither
they summoned me through Bucer, saying
that Glapion had something about which he
wished to treat secretly with me. All this
the Archbishop of Mainz arranged, in order
to delay my journey,[2] for but a few days
remained to me of the time allowed by my
safe-conduct. Then I did not know their
frauds. Christ has overcome the cunning
of my adversaries through my simplicity,
for the pope shall be utterly destroyed."

[2] Luther arrived at Worms April 16, 1521, the last day
allowed him by his safe conduct. Had the plot to delay him
succeeded he would not have been able to appear before the
Diet at all.

10. THE CONTROVERSY WITH CARLSTADT, 1523.

When Luther had been summoned by the elector[1] to recall from their insane opinions those whom Carlstadt[2] had corrupted, he came to Kahla, a village of Thuringia. There, in the place where he was to preach, the followers of Carlstadt had placed a crucifix, which they had cut into many pieces in order to show their hatred of it. He said that he was indeed deeply grieved, but, nevertheless, because he saw that it was an insult of the devil, he had gone up and preached without referring to the matter in any way. " I did this," said he " to show the devil that I also could be haughty; for there is no better way to conquer Satan, if he is thus proudly insulting, than to ignore him."

" If Carlstadt believes that there is any God in heaven or earth, may Christ my Lord never be kind nor gracious to me. That is a terrible imprecation, but my reason for

[1] Frederic the Wise, August, 1523.

[2] Andrew Bodenstein of Carlstadt (c. 1480–1541), one of Luther's colleagues at Wittenberg, and an earnest reformer. They fell out over the doctrine of the Real Presence, which Luther asserted and Carlstadt denied.

making it is this: Dr. Carlstadt knows that concerning the bread and wine we do not utter bubbles nor hisses, but that we speak the holy, heavenly words of God Almighty, which Christ himself spoke with his holy mouth at the last supper, and commanded to be spoken. And as Carlstadt knows that we have God's word, and yet dares deliberately to cry out against it, to mock it and laugh it to scorn as a human hissing and blowing, thus destroying the poor people with such lies and poison, and as he shows no fear, hesitation nor remorse at doing so, but only manifests joy and pleasure in such wickedness, how can he believe or think that God exists? He is possessed with devils not a few. Well, let it pass; he will soon find out that there is a God, if he hasn't already. If God doesn't grant him that, then I, too, will say there is no God. But in friendship I warn Dr. Carlstadt to repent; he has delayed long enough, soon a change will come. O dear God, what don't we do when thou lettest us?"[1]

"Carlstadt is a most striking example of hypocrisy. Deserting the university, he moved with all his effects into the country,

[1] This saying was recorded by Erasmus Alber, who heard it at Luther's table in December, 1540. Published in *Archiv fur Reformationsgeschichte*, xi, 141 (1914).

and I have seen him standing in the dung with bare feet, loading manure on a cart, after the manner of the peasants."

"Münzer, Carlstadt and Campanus are very devils incarnate, for they think of nothing except to do harm and revenge themselves."

11. MARRIAGE AND FAMILY LIFE.

"God knows," said Luther, "that I had no thought of going so far in this matter as I have gone. I thought only to attack indulgences. If anyone had told me, when I was at the Diet of Worms: 'In six years you will have a wife and be sitting at home,' I should not have believed it."[1]

To show his approval of marriage Luther said: "Before I was married I had decided that, should I become unexpectedly ill, I should like to have some girl wedded to me on my death bed, in order to confound the pope who has cast down and dishonored this estate more than can be said. He and his impious rules are as bad as Sodom."[2]

Little Hans[3] said gravely as he was sitting at table: "What fun it must be in heaven to eat and jump and play. There is a river of milk there, and nice breakfast rolls grow of themselves." "A child's life is the happiest," said the doctor, "for he has no

[1] Luther said this in 1532, seven years after his marriage and eleven years after the Diet of Worms.
[2] Luther married Catharine von Bora, June 13, 1525.
[3] Luther's eldest son, born June 7, 1526.

[41]

political cares nor ecclesiastical abuses to contend with, nor does he fear death nor future infirmity, but sees only the good."

Once he said to Hans: "How much do you suppose you cost me in a year?" The boy answered: "O father, you don't have to buy the bread and milk, but the apples and pears must cost a lot."[1] "Thus," moralized the doctor, "men despise God's daily gifts, but esteem highly what are really trifles."

"Cruciger's baby was baptized Theodore, but I say that common names are best.[2] Everyone expected a rare name when my eldest son was born; they said I ought to give him a new name as I had brought so many new doctrines into the world."

"My boy Hans is now[3] entering his seventh year. Every seven years a person changes; the first period is infancy, the second childhood. At fourteen they begin to see the world and lay the foundations of education,

[1] The child naively supposed that the milk and bread cost nothing, since the former came from the cow and the latter was made by his mother, doubtless from home-grown wheat. The explanation offered by the editor of the Weimar edition of the Table Talk, that Hans was probably not present when the flour and meat were bought, but was no doubt on hand when the fruit was purchased, seems not to agree with the first sentence of Hans's answer.

[2] The name Theodore was extremely rare in Germany at that time.

[3] June 7, 1532. Luther was then nearly forty-nine.

OIL-PAINTING by Adolph Spanenberg, at Leipzig, representing Luther and his wife and children, Hans, Magdalene, Martin, Paul and Margaret. Melanchthon is also seated at the table.

at twenty-one the young men seek marriage, at twenty-eight they are house-holders and patres-familias, at thirty-five they are magistrates in church and state, until forty-two when they are kings. After that the senses begin to decline. Thus every seven years brings a new condition in body and character, as has happened to me and to us all."

Taking his child Martin[1] the doctor said, " If you become a lawyer I will hang you on the gallows. You must be a preacher, baptize, dispense the sacrament, visit the sick and comfort the sorrowful.

" What cause have you given me to love you so? How have you deserved to be my heir? By making yourself a general nuisance. Do you deserve that we should care for you and get you a nurse? And why aren't you thankful instead of filling the house with your howls? "

As his baby was being taken to bed he said: " Go to sleep, dear little boy. I have no gold to leave you, but a rich God. Only be good."

January 28, 1533, in the first hour of the night, a third son was born to Dr. Martin Luther whom he called Paul. His sponsors were the most illustrious Duke John Ernest,

[1] Born November 9, 1531.

John Löser, Jonas, Melanchthon and the wife of Caspar Lindener. Luther greeted Löser as he came up with the words: "I am troubling you again, sir. Today a new pope has been born; you will help the poor fellow to his rights." After the child had been baptized he invited the sponsors to dinner, and I, Lauterbach, served the meal. They talked in most friendly wise, and among other things Luther said: "I have called him Paul, for St. Paul has given me many a good saying and argument, wherefore I wished to honor him. May God give him grace! I will send my children away to educate them, one to be a soldier with Löser, one to study with Jonas and Melanchthon and one to work with some peasant."

"Weeds grow fast; therefore girls grow faster than boys."

On Sunday, March 3, 1538, Luther held a symposium of his kingdom. Songs were sung and every one recited a Psalm or gospel text or some of the catechism or a prayer as he was asked. Sometimes they hesitated through timidity. He said: "What will happen at the last judgment when impious men are openly condemned and have to plead their cause? The majesty of that judgment is great and all men are compelled

to dread it. Let the wicked prosper here
in their presumption and contumacy; they
must all await that judgment. There all
their glory will vanish and the thoughts of
all men and of Satan himself will be published.
Therefore not without reason do Paul and
the other apostles confidently await this
judgment of the wicked." Then a servant
recited a verse from Psalm cx, "The Lord
hath sworn and will not repent, 'Thou art
a priest forever after the order of Mel-
chizedek.'" The doctor said: "That is the
fairest and noblest verse in the whole Psaltery, where God sets forth this Christ, who
alone deserves to be a bishop and supreme
pontiff, and none other but he. It cannot be Caiaphas nor Annas, nor Peter
nor Paul, but he and he alone will be
priest. That I swear, that he alone shall
be priest; therefore flee to him. I remember
the use made of this text in the Epistle to
the Hebrews."[1]

"He who takes a wife ought to be a good

[1] There is diversity in the reading of this text. That of
Meyer: *Ueber Lauterbachs und Aurifabers Sammlungen der
Tischreden Luthers*, p. 38, is here followed in preference to
that given in Seidemann: *Lauterbachs Tagebuch auf das Jahr
1538*, p. 44f, notwithstanding the fact that Professor G.
Kawerau, in an article in the *Theologische Literaturzeitung*,
supports Seidemann. The incident will remind the reader
of Burns's poem: "The Cotter's Saturday Night."

man, but Hans Metzsch[1] is not worthy of this divine gift, for a good woman deserves a good husband. To have peace and love in marriage is a gift which is next to the knowledge of the Gospel. There are heartless wretches who love neither their children nor their wives; such beings are not human.

" The greatest blessing is to have a wife to whom you may entrust your affairs and by whom you may have children. Katie, you have a good husband who loves you. Let another be empress, but you give thanks to God."[2]

" The faith and life of young children are the best because they have simply the Word. We old fools have hell and hell-fire; we dispute concerning the Word, which they accept with pure faith without question; and yet at the last we must hold simply to the Word as they do. It is moreover a trick of the devil, that we are drawn by our business affairs away from the Word in such a manner that we do not know ourselves how it happens. Therefore it is best to die young."

[1] Hans Metzsch was bailiff of Wittenberg. On another occasion Luther said of him: "I have excommunicated my captain on account of his immorality, and I am unwilling that he should participate in our sacraments."

[2] Another report of Luther's conversation has it that he said to his wife: "You are an empress; recognize it and thank God."

To his infant child Luther said: " You are our Lord's little fool. Grace and remission of sins are yours and you fear nothing from the law. Whatever you do is uncorrupted; you are in a state of grace and you have remission of sins, whatever happens."

Playing with his child, Magdalene, he asked her: " Little Lena, what will the Holy Christ give you for Christmas? "[1] And then he added: " The little children have such fine thoughts about God, that he is in heaven and that he is their God and father; for they do not philosophize about him."

As Magdalene lay in the agony of death,[2] her father fell down before the bed on his knees and wept bitterly and prayed that God might free her. Then she departed and fell asleep in her father's arms. Her mother was also in the room but farther from the bed because of her grief.

As they laid her in the coffin he said: " Darling Lena, it is well with you. You will rise and shine like a star, yea like the sun. . . . I am happy in spirit but the flesh is sorrowful and will not be content; the

[1] This was shortly before Christmas, 1531, when Magdalene was about two and a half years old.
[2] September 20, 1542.

parting grieves me beyond measure. It is strange that she is certainly in peace and happy and yet I so sorrowful. . . . I have sent a saint to heaven.

"We should care for our children, and especially the poor little girls. I do not pity boys; they can support themselves in any place if they will only work, and if they are lazy they are rascals. But the poor little race of girls must have a staff to lean upon. A boy can go to school and become a fine man if he will. But a girl cannot learn so much and may turn to shame to get bread to eat."

As his wife was still sorrowful and wept and cried aloud, he said to her: "Dear Katie, think how it is with her, and how well off she is. But flesh is flesh and blood blood and they do as their manner is; the spirit lives and is willing. Children doubt not, but believe as we tell them; all is simple with them; they die without pain or anguish or doubt or fear of death just as though they were falling asleep."

"Aunt Lena[1] would you like to go back to the convent?" "No, indeed," she re-

[1] Magdalene von Bora, Catharine's aunt, who had been a nun with her at Nimbschen came to live at the Black Cloister after her niece's marriage to Luther.

plied. Then mistress Felicitas von Selmenitz asked her why she did not want to go back. Luther said: "And I ask, in general, why women do not want to remain unmarried?" No one answered but all laughed.

Speaking of female beauty Luther recalled what Martin Bucer had said:[1] "Doctor, our women would be pretty if their coloring were not misplaced. They have fine red eyes, pale white lips, yellow teeth and black necks, whereas they ought to have red cheeks, white faces and black eyebrows." While he was saying this three youths, one of whom was George Kaufmann,[2] came in drunk, holding in their hands goblets, and drinking to lute-players and other youths who preceded them. Dr. Martin Luther looked at them sternly and said: "Drink until some misfortune befall you! Such as you will never reach old age, for the best part of mankind perishes by drinking too

---

[1] Luther speaks on some day between October 28 and December 12, 1536 (Kroker, *Luthers Tischreden in der Mathesischen Sammlung,* no. 707c). Bucer had been in Wittenberg during the last days of May at the time the Wittenberg Agreement was drawn up, and had dined with Luther on May 27. It was doubtless at that time that the conversation here recalled took place. *Cf.* Smith, *Luther,* p. 294.

[2] Luther's nephew, an orphan, who, with his brothers and sisters, was long sheltered by the Reformer.

much. I was lately at court preaching right fiercely against drink, but it does no good. Taubenheim and Minckewitz said that it could not be otherwise at court, and that music and all knightly games had declined and only drinking was honored. And our elector,[1] a really robust man, can stand a lot of drinking. What is necessary to satisfy his natural thirst is enough to make his neighbor drunk. . . . If I go again to see the prince, I will certainly request him to command all his subjects everywhere to swill themselves full; perhaps if they are required to drink, they won't, for, as Ovid says, ' We strive for the forbidden and desire what we may not have.' "

February 22 (1538) the doctor's wife complained of the disobedience of the servants. He replied: " They are so bad that they need a ruler like the Turk who could treat them as they deserve, and measure out for them, day by day, their work and rations as Pharaoh did to the children of Israel in the Exodus. Such disobedience provokes God's wrath and tempts him to send us the Turk."

" ' Give and it shall be given unto you.' That is a true saying which makes the world

[1] John Frederic, elector 1532–47.

rich and poor. Those who give nothing, thinking to leave more to their children, keep nothing. Poverty comes upon them, as has happened to many rich men and will happen again. Misers and Turks lay up riches for their children but the proverb shall come true, ' the third heir shall not enjoy badly gotten gain.' Contrariwise to him who gives shall be given. My house observes that rule. I will not boast but I know what I give each year in my house. Chancellor Brück said: 'If the elector gave him a noble's income, his household could not stand the strain of his liberality, and yet he has only three hundred gulden a year! But God gives enough and blesses it, and I also will give. Dear Katie, if we are ever out of money we must sell our cups; we must keep giving if we want anything more."

" God is the protector and provider of the poor, as I, who spend more than my salary, certainly experience. I have never written, preached, nor taught for pay, for the two hundred gulden[1] given me by the elector are a free gift. Who has Christ has enough.

[1] Luther's salary prior to his marriage in 1525 was 100 gulden ($50 or £10) and his board; it was then raised to 200; in 1532 to 300 and in 1536 to 400, apparently the regular salary of a professor. Luther had, in addition, his house, and many gifts and pensions. *Cf.* Smith, *Luther*, 366ff.

Wherefore I would never work for money, though I might as well have become rich had I wished to make as much as possible."

"God has given me all things without price. The printers offered me four hundred gulden per annum for my manuscripts, but I declined them, not wishing to sell God's free gifts. God has wonderfully saved me from that snake the papacy; if I have been scratched the pope has not escaped with a whole skin but has been tolerably well beaten. I have enough, and thank God who has given me a wife and children, that fair blessing; and the elector who voluntarily gives me three hundred[1] gulden per annum. Formerly I said that after I had married I would take money for lecturing, but as God anticipated my need through the elector I have never sold a manuscript nor lectured for money my whole life long, and I will go to the grave with this boast, ' having food and raiment, therewith to be content.' "

"If I live another year my poor little room[2] must go, the one from which I stormed

[1] Text "two hundred," one of the many mistakes of the note-takers. The saying was said on July 1, 1539, when Luther was receiving three hundred gulden cash and one hundred in kind. In 1540 he reckons his income now at three, now at four hundred.

[2] Luther speaks in 1532. Extensive alterations were made in the Black Cloister on account of the fortifications erected

[52]

the papacy and which is on that account
worthy of perpetual memory. But the
cannon and fortifications and princes eat it
away from me, for they persuade the elector
to do it. They hate us so heartily that they
tried to prevent the young prince[1] from studying, saying: 'Gracious Lord, why should
he need great learning? Are you going to
make a clerk out of him?' For they feared
that if taught he would read history and so
see their wiles. With these crafty words
the Elector Frederic[2] could not be moved.
They are doubly possessed of the seven deadly
sins, and their malice surpasses all malice.
Ernest von S——— is a merchant; is that,
too, noble? They are all malicious; is that
Christian?

"Great houses, as the Elector Frederic
once said, mean great cares, small houses,
small cares, and so those who are ambitious
to live in large houses do not realize that
they are preparing trouble for themselves."

by the electors in the wall near by. *Cf.* Smith, *Luther*, p. 364.
Kroker located the little room in the high passage-way then
existing between the main building and the outhouses east of
it. It is possible, however, that it was in a tower between
the Cloister and the town wall to the west. *Cf.* Grisar,
Luther, i, 319ff, and Smith, *Luther's Correspondence*, i, 183.

[1] John Frederic, who succeeded his father John in August,
1532.

[2] John Frederic's uncle, elector until May, 1525.

When Luther's wife was lamenting the fact that there were only three bottles of beer left, he said to her: "That doesn't matter so long as the head of the family is God, who can easily make four out of three."

"God denied to women all authority in public affairs, as we see, because they have not the strength for office in either the state or the church."

"Women have by nature the art of speech, which men acquire only by great industry. But it is in household affairs that this is true; in public life this rhetorical ability does not avail. For *that*, men have been created, not women."

"My advice to all who wish to marry is that they should not treat the matter as a joke. And do not follow simply the inclinations of the flesh, but pray, pray. For once having taken a wife, it is not permitted to draw back if the affair should turn out badly; for the wife given in marriage is herself a dowry. Simply pray, for it is necessary. If moreover the wife should be disagreeable, she must be borne with, for she belongs in the home."

"If I had to marry again, I would hew me an obedient wife out of stone; for I despair of the obedience of all other women."

" Satan plots incessantly to destroy con-
jugal happiness, for he knows it is a great
gift."

When one day Luther's wife was upholding
her authority pretty insistently he said to
her with feeling: " You may claim for yourself the control over the affairs of the house,
saving, nevertheless, my just rights. Female
government has accomplished no good since
the world began. When God constituted
Adam master of all creatures, they were safe
and governed in the best way, but the inter-
vention of woman spoiled all; for that we
have you women to thank, and therefore I
am not willing to endure your rule."

" Poor people who marry in God's name
and become rich are much more numerous
than rich people who marry for money and
remain rich. Mörlin's father[1] marries a
poor but handsome girl for love, though he
hasn't even bread in the house. Now God
bestows on him a good living and has given
him fine children, for God thinks: ' It is my
ordinance, I must give him enough.' I, too,
had nothing, and afterwards I wished to
write and teach without pay, but God bestowed on me four hundred gulden [per

---

[1] Jodocus Mörlin, father of Joachim, had been professor
of metaphysics in Wittenberg; at this time (1540) he was
pastor in Westhausen. Kroker, *op. cit.*, p. 178.

annum]. At that time I had a salary of about five and a half dollars,[1] but the inspectors took it away from me and gave me nothing else."

" Among the Jews every man had to marry about the age of nineteen; few or none were permitted to wait till the twentieth year. Benjamin had ten sons, but not his daughter, before his thirty-third year, when he moved into Egypt. Therefore the number of the people was great, and they lived close to one another. They trusted much to numbers, and on that account had to marry early. The bearing of children they held in high esteem. Our women simply detest the bringing of children into the world, for the reason that they dislike the trouble of rearing and educating them and prefer a life of ease. We see in comedies that among the Greeks also there was love of progeny. Among the Jews it was not only a shame not to have children, but there was also the fear of God's wrath. Therefore Elizabeth held it for such a great blessing that the reproach of being barren had been removed from her."[2]

When Luther's father was asked by Coelius, the preacher at Mansfeld, whether he

[1] 9 alte schock. An altes schock seems to have been a sum of money about equal to sixty cents.
[2] Luke i, 25.

believed in those things which are presented
to us in the confession of faith, he answered:
" He must be a scoundrel who would not
believe that." Luther: " That reminds one
of the old days [of unquestioning faith]! "—
Melancthon: " Happy are they who thus
die in the knowledge of Christ, as your
Magdalene has already died. For the older
we grow the more foolish we grow, which is
proved by the fact that the younger people
cling with simplicity to the articles of faith;
as they learned them so they believe them.
But when we become old, then we begin to
dispute; we try to be clever, but we are
nevertheless the greatest fools."

" The human heart," said Luther, " is
able to bear neither good nor bad fortune.
If we have enough money and material goods,
then there is no rest; if we are in poverty,
then there is no joy. Midway between
these extremes, however, there is happiness,
which is to be content with one's lot."

" I am richer than all the papal theologians
in the whole world, for I am contented with
what I have. I have three children[1] born in
honorable wedlock, which no papal theologian
has. Again I am richer than all the nobles
in the land, although I rob my gracious

[1] Hans, Magdalene and Martin. This was in 1532.

[57]

prince, in order that I may be of use to others."[1]

" I dislike to write letters, but whoever gets one from me is likely to have me for a good friend. Thus Queen Mary[2] said to the youth who brought to her a letter from me: ' I see that Dr. Martin Luther likes me.' "

" I think all day long that I am dying, and still I can't die. Who will free me from this mortal body? "[3]

" Nothing tastes good to me any more, neither food nor drink. I am already dead. If I were only buried! "

" The papists are longing eagerly for my death. But when I am dead, then my real life will begin; for the seed does not spring up, till first it has fallen to the ground."

When an excellent medicine was given to Luther for the relief of his head, he replied: " My best prescription is written in the third chapter of John: ' For God so loved the world, that he gave his only begotten son, that whosoever believeth in him should not perish, but have everlasting life.' That is the best medicine that I have."

[1] Luther frequently begged the elector to help others, but he never asked anything for himself.

[2] Mary of Hungary. Luther dedicated to her some Consolatory Psalms, November 1, 1526. Enders, v, 402f., DeWette, iii, 132f.

[3] This was in 1532, fourteen years before his death.

At another time Luther said: "I am so ill! But no one believes it, nor will, till I go the way of all the others. Now, dear Lord, you had me when I was well, you must also have me when I am sick; as wives say to their husbands: 'You had me when I was young, so you must have me now that I am old.'"

"Many good things come from a wife: the blessing of the Lord, children, community of all things and other things so good that they might overwhelm a man. Suppose there were no women, not only the house and household but even the state would perish. Even if we could beget children without women we could not get along without them."

"Mere lust is felt even by flees and lice; love begins when we wish to serve others."

Anthony Lauterbach told Dr. Luther that the Archbishop of Mainz thought ill of his call to the diaconate, saying that he was a layman, not yet consecrated by orders. Anthony had replied to the archbishop's officer that he had been ordained through his wife,[1] for they were one body. Luther called this an excellent answer to that prelate.

[1] Lauterbach married a nun named Agnes in 1533, the same year in which he was given the position of deacon, first at Leisnig and then at Wittenberg.

Then he told a story about a husband who, after heavily eating and drinking mocked his hungry wife, saying: "Aren't you satisfied? I have done nothing but eat and drink the whole day, and didn't you taste it? Are we not one body?" The next day she stayed away the whole day, eating and drinking, but preparing nothing for him, and when he returned derided him with the same words, "Man and wife are one body."

Martin Luther gazed at the painting[1] of his wife, and said: "I will have a husband painted for it, and send it to Mantua[2] asking whether they prefer marriage or celibacy." Then he began to commend marriage as a divine institution, from which all things flow, and without which the world would be empty, and all creatures useless since they were made on man's account. "Therefore were it not for Eve and her breasts, no other institution could have followed. Inspired by the Holy Ghost Adam called his wife by a splendid name, Eve, that is, mother; he did not say 'woman,' but 'mother,' and added 'of all living.'[3] Here

[1] Lucas Cranach painted Catharine Luther in 1525, and several times later. One of these pictures doubtless hung on the wall.

[2] I.e., to the Council summoned to meet at Mantua in 1537, to which the Lutherans were invited.

[3] Genesis, iii, 20.

*P*ORTRAIT *of CATHERINE LUTHER*
By Cranach. Original in Milan.

you have the glory of woman, namely that she is the fountain of all living men. The words were short, but such an oration as Demosthenes and Cicero never composed, for it is an oration of the most eloquent Holy Ghost, and worthy of our first parent. He it is who thus declaims, and when such an orator speaks and praises, we may well connive at all in which a woman fails. Christ the Saviour did not despise her, but entered into her womb. To this Paul alludes when he says, ' A woman shall be saved by child-bearing.' "[1]

" The highest grace of God is that love should always be strong in marriage. The first love is fervid, a drunken love, blinding us and leading us on;[2] but when we sleep off our drunkenness, then, if good, we have the sincere love of marriage, but if evil, we rue it."

With a sigh Dr. Martin said: " Dear God! What a bother all these matrimonial cases are to us! Great as is the trouble and labor of getting people together, it is far harder to keep them together. Adam's fall has vitiated our nature and made it most fickle. It runs hither and thither like quick-

[1] 1 Tim., ii, 15.
[2] "Hinan," the same word and thought used by Goethe in his famous: "Das Ewig-weibliche zieht uns hinan."

silver. How fine it is when married people only keep together at bed and board! If they do murmur at each other now and then, that is the accompaniment of matrimony. Adam and Eve must have scolded each other roundly during their nine hundred years, as, 'You ate the apple,' and, 'But you gave it to me!' I doubt not that during so long a life infinite evils happened to them as they sighed over their fall. It must have been an extraordinary régime! In fact Genesis is a wonderful book of wisdom and reason."

"After Lucas the artist[1] had taken his wife and the wedding had been held, he was always desirous of being next the bride. Now he had a good friend, who said to him: 'Friend, do not do that! Before six months are gone, you will have enough of that! There will not be a maid in the house, that you will not prefer to your wife.' And so it is. We hate those things that are present and love those that are absent. As Ovid says: 'What we may have, we do not care for; 'tis what we may not have that rouses keen desire.'[2] That is the weakness of our nature. For the devil then comes and throws

[1] The reference is to Lucas Cranach the Younger (1515–1586), who married the daughter of Chancellor Brück in 1541.

[2] Amores, 2, 19, 3.

in the way hatreds, suspicions, concupiscence on both sides, and then desertion follows. To get a wife is easy enough, but to love her with contsancy is difficult, and he who can do that may well be grateful to our Lord God. Therefore if any one wants to marry a wife, let him take the matter seriously and pray to our Lord God: ' O Lord, if it is thy divine will that I should live without a wife, then help me to do so! If not, bestow upon me a good, pious maid, with whom I can live my whole life long, one whom I love and who loves me.' For the mere union of the flesh is not sufficient. There must be congeniality of tastes and character."

The doctor said: " Our Lord God gives every time more than we ask. When we ask only for a piece of bread, he gives us a whole acre.[1] I asked God to permit my Katie to live,[2] and he gives her a good year in addition. But I think another visitation of the plague will follow, for we are too wicked, and heresy has broken out among us."

" I have privately permitted some married people who have as wife or husband a leprous

[1] Luther had just purchased from his brother-in-law the farm of Zulsdorf, near Leipzig.

[2] Katie had recently suffered a severe illness due to a miscarriage.

person to marry in addition some one else, but only on this condition, that the leprous spouse be supported. For some medicine must be found for consciences. The pope provides for separation, lest the poison spread, but does not allow another marriage."[1]

He spoke much of the arrogance and negligence of artisans, who had little diligence and high wages. " I have cloth enough, but cannot get any trousers made. I have myself patched this pair four times, and will patch them again before I have a new pair made. For the tailors have no care; they take much material but give it no shape. Thus in Italy they have done well, where the tailors have a special guild of trouser makers. But here they pattern hose, breeches and coat all on the same form."

Speaking of the ingratitude of his brothers and kinsmen who dealt unjustly with him in dividing his inheritance,[2] he said: " If they

[1] This shows that Luther countenanced bigamy under certain circumstances, though he refused to allow complete divorce.

[2] Hans Luther, the Reformer's father, dying May 29, 1530, left about 1500 gulden, or $750, worth in purchasing power twenty times as much. After the death of Luther's mother, June 30, 1531, there was an unfortunate quarrel about the division of the estate, which was finally settled amicably on July 10, 1534, by assigning to each of the five children, or their heirs, an equal part in the property.

do this while I am alive, what will they do to my children after my death? I wish that they had kept the three hundred florins, my inheritance, in the name of all the devils. God gives me more than this. I spend more in a year than my heritage. God, who considers me his servant, supports me well, as he has proved up till now. To him, as to a Father, I commend my children. That shall be their great treasure. And my son will be rich when my kinsmen are begging."

12. HOW THE TABLE TALK WAS COLLECTED.

I[1] wrote in my note-book: "Luther to Melanchthon: 'You are an orator in writing but not in speaking,'" for the candor of both speaker and listener pleased me. Melanchthon wanted to persuade Luther not to answer a pamphlet published by the parson at Cölln,[2] who, Luther said, was "the assassin of Dresden." But what I wrote did not please Melanchthon, and after he had asked me again and again for the note-book in which I was accustomed to write what I heard, at length I gave it to him, and when he had read a little he wrote this couplet:

"All things, Cordatus, do not try to tell,
A decent silence upon some were well."

Indeed I always knew that it was an audacious offence to write down all that I heard when I stood before the table or sat at it as guest, but the utility of the practice conquered my shame, and moreover the

[1] Conrad Cordatus. *Cf. supra*, introduction. P. xf.
[2] Arnoldi, pastor of a little town (not Cologne) in Duke George's dominions. Luther was inclined to attribute his work to Duke George, "the assassin of Dresden." Cordatus did not perfectly understand the situation of which he wrote.

doctor never showed even by a word that what I did displeased him. Nay more, I made way for others, especially Veit Dietrich and John Schlaginhaufen; I hope to incorporate their notes with mine, which would make many pious men my debtors. I wish to add this explanation, because I was confounded by Philip's poetry, and no one imitates us now.[1] Let whoever copies these notes even if he does it against my will, at least do it with the same simple, candid spirit in which I have written them, and let him prize Luther's words, as I do, more than the oracles of Apollo. I report not only his *dicta* on theology and other serious matters, but also, as an ornament for the rest, his jocose and casual remarks.

Our God sent me[2] this year to Luther's table, through the request of Jonas and Rörer, for which I thank my God and these friends my whole life long. What I saw and heard there I diligently remarked, and God gave me many good sayings reported by

[1] Cordatus evidently added this later, perhaps in 1537 when he copied his notes.

[2] Mathesius speaks in 1540. On him and his companions whom he mentions just below, *cf. supra*, introduction. P. xiiif. This passage is from his *Historien von D. M. Luthers Anfang, Lehr, Leben und Sterben*, cap. xii.

Dietrich, Weller, Lauterbach, Heydenreich,
Besold, Plato and other boarders of the
doctor. Ferdinand a Maugis, an Austrian,
noted much in his Bible and Rörer took
much precious material on the interpretation of Scripture. As our doctor often took
weighty and deep thoughts with him to table,
sometimes during the whole meal he would
maintain the silence of the cloister, so that
no word would be spoken; nevertheless at
suitable times he let himself be very merry,
so that we were accustomed to call his sayings
the condiments of the meal, which were pleas-
anter to us than all spices and delicate food.
If he wished to get us to speak he would
make a beginning: "What's the news?"
The first time we let the remark pass, but
if he said again: "Ye prelates, what's the
news in the land?" then the older men would
begin to talk. Doctor Wolfgang Schiefer,
a travelled man of the world who had been
preceptor to his Roman Majesty's[1] children,
was often the first to introduce a subject,
unless there was a stranger present. If the
conversation was animated, it was nevertheless conducted with decent propriety and
courtesy, and the others would not take
their turn at it until the doctor spoke. Often

[1] *I.e.* Ferdinand, King of the Romans, brother of Charles V.

good questions of the Bible would be propounded, which he solved finely, satisfactorily and concisely, and if any one took exception to any part he would even suffer that and refute him courteously.

13. CONTEMPORARY POLITICS.

" The Diet of Augsburg[1] did not do what our opponents wished; I hope and shall pray God that the present Diet[2] may do as little. Duke George has written a stout memorial which he thinks he will take with him to the Diet. I wish the emperor would make him pope. I think he would soon make the bishops who have many dioceses but who agree with Luther in other things, see that they would rather follow Luther than Pope George. He wishes to reform their pluralism and they won't have it."

" Pope Clement is the richest of all men and yet the most miserable. He is a thorough scoundrel and works much mischief. He says that before he is through he will have the Turk at our throats and so he will. Therefore pray diligently and think of it when I am dead, for the pope has many wicked plans as has King Ferdinand, yet neither of them succeeds. There is no greater rascal than Clement except Satan. He plans trouble for me but will not get ahead of me. His plots stop at nothing. He tried

[1] 1530. *Cf.* Smith, *Luther,* 247ff.
[2] January, 1532, Smith, p. 275.

to ruin the Roman Empire and made a treaty with the king of France, but was smitten at Pavia.[1] And now his plan of setting the Turk on us will fail. He is a Florentine bastard."

"Duke George is away at the Diet of Ratisbon.[2] He will not rest until he is Elector of Saxony, a title to which he has no right. So he went early to the Diet to disturb the peace. How he will rage and eat his heart out when peace is made! I am pleased at his trouble, for he only regrets that he cannot revenge himself and satisfy his lust for doing harm. He has worked up such a hatred against us, that, if he cannot digest it, he will die of it. He will die of vexation at not being able to do harm."

"Duke George will never think that God remembers his own. He sins against the Holy Ghost and belongs in the abyss of hell. The good, pious emperor hurt him sorely by keeping the peace, so he has begun to persecute his own people.

"They say a mad dog lives only nine days, but Duke George has been mad nine years. He will be a lunatic soon. He has just ex-

[1] King Francis I of France was defeated by the emperor at Pavia, February 24, 1525.

[2] January, 1532, Smith, p. 275.

[71]

iled some of his subjects on account of the sacrament."

"Noble are the Elector John Frederic and the Landgrave Philip, who are burdened with public not private cares. If they live ten years longer (though it is hard to see how they can when they are so pressed), it will be a good thing for posterity. Our elector is watchful; the host is at home. He works from early morning until noon, and writes cunningly. He is not given to drink,[1] women, avarice nor gaming, but is diligent, pious and liberal. Our God will maintain him. When I was in Torgau with the Archbishop of Mainz and the Margrave of Brandenburg I preached against the shameful drunkenness of the courtiers who might take a good example from our elector."

Luther — Our Lord God must reckon drunkenness a daily sin of us Germans for we can't leave it, although it is a shameful plague destructive to body, soul and estate.

Schiefer — Doctor, they say that at court you never attacked this vice.

Luther — Indeed I often did, and in the presence of the whole court. Truly I called

[1] John Frederic was sometimes accused of too great fondness for the bottle; Luther himself says so occasionally.

it a filthy, scurvy vice of the nobles by which they led the elector astray and hurt him much. Such teaching pleased the late elector well, for he lived soberly and often allowed John Frederic to stay at table until seven o'clock. But my words did no good. I said to the nobles: "After dinner you ought to have a wrestling bout or some such exercise; then I would allow you a good carouse, for drunkenness may be borne once in a while, but not as a steady habit." Then the wife of Dr. Leonard Stetner related that Luther had said in his sermon: "You look in the morning as if your heads had soaked in salt water."

" We certainly have a prince [John Frederic] adorned with many gifts. He has a reverent tongue and listens to no base or blasphemous word. He loves the Bible, schools and churches; he carries a heavy burden and alone keeps the faith. . . . He would gladly attend to everything but he cannot. His only vice is that he drinks too much with his friends and perhaps builds too much. But he works like a donkey. If we didn't pray earnestly for him we should not do right."

On February 17 (1538), the doctor dined with Pucher and other notable strangers.

Terrible things were said of the Archbishop of Mainz who was hard pressed for money and infamous besides. He could not borrow on his seal and signature. He paid fifteen per cent yearly for loans. He had hypothecated and sold jewels, pictures and lands. Luther said: " Such a scoundrel deserves a great curse for having had his preacher George Winkler assassinated and for having hung John Schenitz, notwithstanding the inhibition of the emperor and the offer of Schenitz's friends to give 80,000 gulden not for acquittal but simply for a just trial. I hope the prelate will yet be called to account for stringing up Schenitz. It was treachery which God the just judge will avenge with the brand of infamy. Wherefore I wrote a letter with my own hand and sent it to the archbishop[1] saying: If thieves are to be hanged the Archbishop of Mainz should first of all be hanged on a gallows seven times as high as the Giebichenstein.[2] I also spoke much of his mistress Elsa whom he had despoiled of her jewels and had bound. Once at Lisk he had her put into

[1] The letter of January, 1536 is meant, Enders, x. 296; De Wette, iv, 676. On Schenitz, Smith, *Luther*, 297f.

[2] A fortress, now in ruins, on the outskirts of Halle, where Schenitz was hanged at the order of Albert, Archbishop Elector of Mainz.

a casket and carried into the cloister like a holy relic. He has since fallen on misfortune. He fears neither God nor men."

July 1 (1538), Luther sighed and said: "Dear Lord Jesus Christ, give me life and strength and I will shave that parson's[1] head, for he is wicked and a crafty mocker of all men. All other princes are rustics compared to him. He is bold indeed and dares to boast that few of his attempts have failed, as though he had dealings with Satan. During the trial of John Schenitz he retained all the lawyers to prevent him having any. They were all timid and did not dare to live up to their professions and follow the example of Papinian.[2] One must speak loud to such a youth as the cardinal, or he will not hear. When I wrote him so severely he could pass over all my charges except this one that he had robbed the poor harlot Elsa of her money. He took it ill that this was published. But that woman died in most pious wise, as Christ says, ' The publicans and harlots go into the kingdom of God before you.' "

[1] *I.e.* Albert of Mainz.

[2] A celebrated Roman jurist, put to death by Caracalla for refusing to write an apology for this emperor's murder of his brother.

(The following conversation took place during the negotiations of 1539. *Cf.* Smith, *Luther*, 314f.)

Melanchthon. It is a devilish thing suitable to the genius of the men of Meissen (I beg Dr. Cruciger's pardon) that they prepared for this war so long ago.

Luther. The victory does not depend on which side has the largest population or the best arms but only on who has the best cause when they meet.

Melanchthon. Our elector sees well what their purpose is, namely to suppress him and destroy our country.

Luther. The prayers of the righteous avail much, as David says. Therefore I prayed. Only let us pray, for the victory will not be won by arms or counsel, but only by prayer.

Melanchthon. They will have plenty to do when they meet; I hear that Carlowitz and Pistorius love calumny and cavilling.

Luther. Let them be as eloquent as they please; as they have begun the matter without us they can finish it without us. Chancellor Brück has often said that Maurice [Duke of Albertine Saxony] was not favorable to us and that we should look out for him.

Melanchthon. What a scandal they have raised!

Luther. True, but what can we do? We can't prevent it.

Melanchthon. They know it at Rome; the pope will write to congratulate the emperor on it. The King of England will know it and the court of Paris will cry out that the house of Saxony is divided against itself and therefore destroying itself.

Luther. True. The devil is having a celebration. He has brought the news to Rome long ago and the papists are laughing in their sleeves.

Melanchthon. Yes, indeed. They will say: "See what our Evangelical friends have come to; see the good fruit of their doctrine!"

Luther. Yes, they will say at Rome that we are coming to blows and will root out our own doctrine. We must listen to such words but God will do what is right. Only pray diligently without doubting and God will bring it to pass. I prayed Duke George to death; we shall laugh Carlowitz and Pistorius to death; God grant that the authors of this treachery end as Judas and Ahitophel did. . . . Duke Maurice is a young man who has little intelligence; he trusts his councillors, but will learn by experience, for no one will trust him in future.

"Melanchthon is a man of authority and weight. He expresses much in few words. We can understand from his letter that there will be war because the papists will not and we cannot yield any thing. I hope it may turn out well, and so commit the cause to God. I shall let him rule while I play the part of Crito in the comedy. We shall pray God to change our adversaries, for we have a good, just cause. Who would not fight for holy things? Even from a political standpoint we are right, for we seek peace which they refuse. That poltroon of Mainz brings misfortune, and the Duke of Brunswick tries to do evil, wherefore our friends must be careful what they say. Delay is unnecessary, for we should anticipate the duke rather than be anticipated by him. If I were in the place of the Landgrave of Hesse I should either punish or destroy those who would not have peace in a just cause. If they really want peace why don't they grant it at once instead of waiting so many days. This letter[1] was written ten days ago, it is now decided. May God the eternal give us his grace. Let us watch and pray, for Satan does not sleep."

[1] *I.e.* from Melanchthon; perhaps the letter of March 3, 1539 (Enders, xii, 106) is meant. On the Peace of Frankfort *cf*. Smith, *Luther*, pp. 314f.

"I do not believe that Henry VIII is human, but the devil incarnate, for besides his other crimes he has now by a fourth[1] murder executed Chancellor Cromwell, his Dr. Brück,[2] whom a few days before he had made judge of his kingdom. Let the devil serve great lords! And this scoundrel asked of us that we should make him the head of our religion, but the elector was unwilling; for we have not yet learned what faith he holds."

"The Elector Frederic was timid about punishing, saying: 'Yes, it is easy to take life, but we cannot restore it.' And Elector John always connived at the deeds of criminals, saying, 'Perhaps they will yet become good.' And so by this leniency they filled the land with rascals. But the prince and magistrate must not be merciful, for consider how harsh is the law of God the all-merciful, when he said: 'He that curseth his father or his mother shall be put to death before the altar.'[3] Off with his head! lest the land be filled with the wicked."

[1] The news of Cromwell's execution, which took place in July, 1540, had apparently just reached Wittenberg. More, Fisher and Anne Boleyn had already been put to death.

[2] Luther means that Cromwell occupied a position in England similar to that of Chancellor Brück in the Electorate of Saxony.

[3] Exodus xxi, 17, quoted from memory.

"We have a pious emperor. He has a bolt on his heart, to close up what he wants. He is silent and pious. I fancy he does not speak as much in a year as I do in one day."

They spoke of the wiles of the Archbishop of Mainz, who was so desperate that he could not live in peace and justice, but rejoiced in civil war to make others perish with him. "He is under the same curse as the atheist, who, unable to repent, said: 'It is better to gallop to hell than to jog-trot to heaven.' Thus Albert of Mainz daily provokes God and men."

Then he spoke of a certain noble at Bitterfeld, in whose pond a peasant was drowned. "That noble wished to claim all the goods of the said peasant because he had been drowned in his waters. This claim was strange, unusual and tyrannical, by which the noble wished to add to the affliction of the widow by seizing her goods! This and similar things are the preparation for some future slaughter by the Turk or the emperor, for we can expect as little good from the emperor as from the Turk."

Then he told of the treachery of a certain courtier of the Archbishop of Mainz, who excused his apostacy from the evangelical to the papal church by saying, 'I will put

Christ behind the door for a while until I become rich, and then I will bring him out again.' Thus another atheist said: ' If you are afraid of death you will never become rich.' Such sayings are most impious and deserve the greatest punishment."

Luther and Schneidewein[1] spoke of the alliance[2] of the emperor, the King of France and the pope, and how, as the dauphin, the eldest son of the French King, had died, his second son was now to marry the daughter[3] of Pope Clement. Luther said: " I wonder at the madness of so great a king, who would incestuously[4] marry a bastard's bastard to his son. It goes with his treachery. It will not be unpunished by God, for he who chastized David's adultery must also repay this sin. He will certainly turn their fair show to shame."

In those days (*scil.* May 12ff, 1538) there came from England Remige, a servant of Dr. John Thixtoll,[5] who related many splendid

[1] Thomas Schneidewein, pastor of Juterbok, near Wittenberg.

[2] Luther speaks in January, 1538, referring to the Peace of Cambrai of 1529.

[3] Catharine de' Medici, a niece of Clement VII, married Francis I's second son, later Henry II, in October, 1533.

[4] By ecclesiastical law marriage with a girl who had been contracted to one's brother, is incestuous.

[5] A tolerably prominent reformer, whose name is met with in the *Calendars of State Papers.* On Luther's relations with England, see *English Historical Review*, October, 1910, pp. 656ff.

and wonderful things about that region and kingdom, how with great desire it hoped for the gospel, and that even some of the bishops preached frankly against the horrible abomination of the pope. He said that the names of Wittenberg, Luther and Melanchthon were held high, and that even those who had only been at Wittenberg and could tell something about it, were also touched with honor. He spoke about the most cultivated part of that country, and related the wiles of the monks of Canterbury, who had made an image of the crucifix, which could move its face and lips and nod its head, by means of cords and keys in the back. This had persuaded many men to worship it, but during the last weeks the frauds had been revealed by the visitation[1] of the king, and publicly demonstrated by a bishop in London, and finally this image was carried everywhere through the streets and torn apart. Luther said: "We should keep this image in our memory, like the one of the Virgin with the child Christ in her arms, which our elector has. The Christ can be moved by cords, and, as though he did not wish adorers to

[1] Many such frauds were exposed by the visitation of the monasteries in 1536. They were brought up to London and their mechanism exposed to the crowds. T. M. Lindsay: *The Reformation*, ii, 343f.

look away from him to his mother, when they seek her mediation he stretches out his little arm and moves himself towards the worshipper."

When Luther was asked whether Thomas More[1] had been slain by his king on account of the gospel, he replied: " By no means! For he was a great tyrant against the Evangelical faith, and poured out much blood of its pious adherents. After he had first examined them under a green tree, he would torture them like a hangman with strange instruments and with torments and in dungeons. Finally, having attained the place second to the king, he attacked the king himself, contrary to the decree of the whole kingdom, and for that he paid the penalty."

Hans von Bora had said: " Duke George, God be merciful to him! " To this the doctor added: " Unmerciful! For if he is not in hell, then Caiaphas is not there either, and there is no hell at all. For in him died the greatest persecutor of the gospel, who acted with the most extreme hatred, joined

---

[1] More, who was Lord Chancellor after the fall of Wolsey, was put to death by Henry VIII, July 6, 1535, for refusing to take the oath of supremacy. He had written a book of unsurpassed virulence against Luther in 1523, and had persecuted the English Lutherans cruelly.

with envy and malice towards his brother. What have his own flesh and blood done to him, that he should wish to disinherit them and give the land to the overlord? When counsellors opposed his plan, he said to them: 'You are unfaithful and betray me!' On that day, when God killed him, he made a will, in which he left all his treasure to the emperor, that the latter might use it against his enemies in Germany; but what enemies has the emperor, except us? He was a wicked, envious man. If he should learn that Duke Henry's[1] children now sit comfortably in his place, it would grieve him in hell. But God is our God. He has him out of the way and three cardinals, and the one at Mainz is very sick. Still when one knave is got rid of, there comes another in his place. The Brunswicker[2] also will not last long."

"Anthony of Schoenberg once said to his brother, the Cardinal Archbishop of Capua: 'You certainly have a bad cause, and in spite of that do you condemn Luther?' But the cardinal, silent at first, at length broke forth: 'Yes, it is too much! It will have to break!' And when he heard that

[1] His brother and successor.
[2] Duke Henry the Younger, of Brunswick-Wolfenbüttel.

at Augsburg[1] we had asked only that we might preach our doctrine without fear, that we were not bound thereby to attack the pope, and that the papists had refused their consent: 'These conditions,' he said, 'ought to have been accepted! For never again will such just terms be offered to the pontiff. I know the character of the Germans.' And," continued Luther, "it will never come so far again, and it ought not to."

When someone said that the King of England had put Doctor Robert Barnes in chains, because he opposed the king's articles, Luther replied: "This king wishes to be God. He establishes articles of faith and prohibits the marriage of the clergy on pain of death, which not even the pope has done. I am something of a prophet; what I prophesy will come to pass; therefore I restrain myself and talk little."

Schiefer said: "If the emperor should grant us peace in our lands for a time, then the business of the assembly[2] would be well done. The doctor added: "Perhaps he will grant it, but on this condition, that we

---

[1] At the Diet of Augsburg, 1530, when the official statement of the Lutheran faith, known as the Augsburg Confession, was presented.
[2] The Conference soon to be held at Hagenau, 1540.

should bar all others from our religion. That we could not do. Let them do it themselves! The Word of God is free, and will not be confined by human decrees.

" Charles is a melancholic voluptuary, with nothing heroic in him. He does not understand our cause, even though he sometimes hears our books read. If he were Scipio or Alexander or Pyrrhus, he would break through the nets of the pope and bind the Germans to himself. He begins many things and finishes few. He took Tunis and has already lost it; he took the French king and let him go; and the same with Rome. He lacks persistence in the conduct of his affairs, and easily gives up, a thing which really able and noble-minded men do not do. What shall I say? Germany is without a head. Melanchthon has compared it to Poliphemus with his eye put out. It is a huge mass, but it lacks a prince! "

" Ferdinand is a monk, observes his seven canonical hours, and neglects the business of the state. Thus Faber[1] will have it; and the emperor must listen to him. He also is ignorant of our doctrine, neither reading it nor hearing it read. This the popes see to, by means of his confessors. They know that

[1] John Faber, Bishop of Vienna.

[86]

our theology is grounded on certainty, and I believe that if the king understood it, he would support it faithfully and drive the pope from Germany. Error and weakness are not such evil diseases as open blasphemy, like that of the Archbishop of Mainz and Duke George. The latter understood our position and said: 'The cause is just, but it has not been approved by the church.' Wherefore the wicked blasphemer is dead and in hell, where he groans away his unworthy existence among the shades."

14. WAR AND TURBULENCE.

" The Swiss argue thus: ' Whoever has a just cause, may rightly make war; we have a just cause, therefore we will make war.' Both premises, major and minor are false and dangerous. For the major premise does not permit wars in general, but only defensive wars; and as to the minor premise, it is open to question whether or not the cause is just. And so the conclusion also is doubtful. Therefore those who say: ' We will have revenge,' rely on human strength; the righteous, however, trust in God: ' For where two or three are gathered together in my name, there am I in the midst of them;'[1] thus to them all things work together for good, while in the case of the papists the reverse is true, since they do not trust in the true God, but in the emperor. Let us stick to prayer, for it is only by praying that we can vex the devil. Our Lord God is a righteous man, let us therefore not forget him."

" If the world were full of concord, peace and justice: if the peasant everywhere were obedient to the prince, the servant to the

[1] Mat. xviii, 20.

master, the wife to the husband, then no one would long for the future life. Therefore God fills this world with turbulence, in order that we may hope for another life!"

15. THE PEASANTS.

As Luther was playing with his infant child he said: "Ah, what a blessing from God children are! Peasants are clearly unworthy of them; they should have pigs only."

"The peasants to-day are evidently swine, and the nobles, who were once unpolluted, are imitating them."

"The disobedience of peasants is unspeakable. They ought therefore to be dealt with most severely by the authorities and the laws. It would not do to abolish serfdom; if the peasants didn't have to work they would go to the devil."

"I am most hostile to all peasants, because, although they enjoy blessings from God and have very few or no temptations to do wrong, they give themselves up to all kinds of sin, even the worst. But who does not love the magistracy, even when it sins, since those in authority are often forced to sin, the more seriously and the oftener in proportion to the greatness of their office, whether in the state or in the church. Tyrants, however, are the vicars of Satan on earth."

Doctor Brück[1] said concerning one of his old peasants, the sliest one of them all and full of deceit, that he had not been able in three years to get him to learn the Lord's prayer; that he himself examined him each year, but yet he did not know it. Doctor Martin replied: " Peasants are beasts! For they think that religion has been invented by us and is not divine. Moreover they take the sacraments mechanically as they wear their clothing. When they are examined, they say: ' Yes, yes!' although they believe nothing. Thus it happened under the papacy, in Dabrun,[2] where a peasant in the agony of death asked for the sacrament, yet was unwilling to believe in the resurrection of the dead; therefore the pastor denied him the sacrament. Then the village magistrate, his godfather, went to him, and tried to persuade him, as follows: ' Dear godson, do believe it, to please me! It won't kill you! I will guarantee that nothing will result from it!' Thus it is evident that neither of them had any faith in this article of the creed."

" A peasant, who is a Christian, is a wooden fire-poker."

[1] Gregory Brück, often called Pontanus (1483 or 1486–1557), at this time chancellor of Electoral Saxony.
[2] Southeast of Wittenberg.

"The princes of the world are gods, the common people are Satan. Through them [the common people] God sometimes brings to pass what otherwise he would accomplish through Satan, namely, seditions, for the punishment of the evil."

"If riches do come to the peasant, he is rather burdened by them than benefited."

"The peasants are not worthy of so many benefits and fruits as they obtain from the earth. I am more grateful to the Lord God for a tree than all the peasants are for all their acres." When Doctor Martin Luther said this, Philip Melanchthon replied: "Doctor, please except some farmers, Adam, Noah, Abraham, Isaac, etc." Luther replied: "They were not only farmers, but also theologians. For the text says of Isaac, in Genesis xxiv, 63: 'And he went out to meditate in the field,' namely, on God's gifts in his creatures."

When Luther's wife brought him some recently hatched chickens, he said: "If farmers appreciated their blessings they would be in paradise. To be in paradise is to know God and to be free from sin, and farmers live in the midst of God's creatures, in which they may see God himself."

"The princes have difficult and extremely

important matters to determine, while the peasants snore in security. If a peasant knew the danger and toil which a prince has to undergo, he would thank God that he is a peasant and in the happiest station in life. But farmers are blind to their own good fortune; they observe only the outward pomp of princes, their clothes, palaces and power, and fail to see that their life is beset, as it were, by fire and flood, while the peasant slumbers peacefully behind the stove. Therefore Elector Frederic, addressing the schoolmaster[1] at Lichtenberg, held that of the various classes in the community the peasants enjoyed the happiest life, for he weighed one after the other the fortunes of all the ranks thus: the emperor was exposed to the greatest perils, calamities and cares; the princes were subject to various hardships; the nobles also had their worries; the burghers, although they had some advantages, had to work for their living. They buy goods with care, expend labor on them, and then sell at a loss; they have to undergo many dangers in winning their daily bread. It is only for the peasants that all things grow of their own accord. To be sure, they pay taxes and tithes, for the land belongs to

[1] Wolfgang Reissenbusch.

the princes; but their labors are most joyful and encouraged by pleasant anticipations. In plowing, planting, sowing, reaping, threshing, wood-cutting — in all this work they look forward to the results with the keenest expectation. It is thus true, as Vergil says: ' Farmers would be extremely happy if they recognized their blessings.'[1] But they are unable to appreciate their good fortune. Men-servants and maid-servants are always better off than their masters and mistresses, because they have no such domestic cares as does the head of the household. My Wolff,[2] my Gretchen,[3] Lena,[4] the servants and attendants are much better off than I and my Katie, for marriage brings with it troubles." Then turning to Veit Dietrich, he said: " If you remain as you are,[5] you will be happy." The latter replied: " I don't wish to remain thus but I shall cast the die, whether I fare better or worse." Luther concluded: " The higher the station, the greater the danger. No one is content with

[1] Vergil, *Georgics*, ii, 485.

[2] Wolfgang Sieberger, Luther's servant.

[3] Perhaps Katie's cook. Aurifaber gives the name as Dorothy.

[4] Probably Magdalene Kaufmann, Luther's niece.

[5] *I.e.*, unmarried. Dietrich at this time was wooing Magdalene Kaufmann. See Introduction, p. xi.

his lot. ' The ox envies the horse, the horse the ox.' "[1]

I[2] said: " Doctor, the common people are offended by the bad morals of the clergy." " What," said he, " do the common people know? They simply want an excuse. We have here upright and honorable men, but what good does it do? If the life of the pastor is bad, then the peasants complain; if good, they say: ' Who can be so good as our pastor? I must look out for myself.' "

" I, Martin Luther, smote all the peasants in their rebellion. For I commanded them to be slain; all their blood is on my head. But I put the responsibility upon our Lord God, who ordered me to say what I did."[3]

[1] Horace, *Epistles*, i, 14, 43. Luther's conversations are remarkable for their wealth of classical allusion. *Cf.* Smith, *Luther*, p. 341.

[2] Mathesius reports this in 1540.

[3] During the peasants' rebellion in 1525 Luther urged the princes to suppress the revolt with ruthless slaughter.

16. SCHOOLS.

" When schools flourish, then things go well and the church is secure. Let us have more learned men and teachers! The youth furnish recruits for the church, they are the source of its well-being. If there were no schools, who would there be to take our places when we die? In the church we are forced to have schools. God has preserved the church through schools, they are its conservatories. They have no fine exterior, but within they are most useful. In schools the children have learned the Lord's prayer and the creed; in the little schools the church has been wonderfully preserved."

" Schoolmasters become bold and learn how to expound the Bible by teaching school. Nowadays young men want to be ordained at once and avoid school work. If one taught school ten years he might retire with a good conscience, for the work is heavy and little honored. In a city a schoolmaster has as much responsibility as a minister. We can take magistrates, princes and nobles as we find them but not schools, for schools rule the world. We see that there is no ruler today who is not of necessity governed by

a lawyer or a minister. The princes know
nothing of themselves and are ashamed to
learn, so they have to apply to the schools.
Were I not a preacher there is no profession
on earth I would sooner follow. One must
not regard how the world esteems and pays
it but how God glorifies it every day."

" It is my opinion that on the last day an
honest schoolmaster will be more honored
than all the popes."

17. MUSIC.

" Music is the greatest gift, indeed it is divine; and therefore Satan is extremely hostile to it, because by its influence many great temptations are overcome. The devil doesn't stay where there is music."

" Music is the highest art, the notes of which cause the words of the text to live. It puts to flight all sad thoughts, as we see in the case of Saul.[1] The nobles think that they have saved our gracious Lord three thousand florins in the matter of music, while they squander in other ways three times as much. Music must be supported by the king and princes, for the preservation of the arts as well as of the laws is the work of monarchs. Private citizens, however much they may love them, are not able to maintain them. Duke George, the Landgrave of Hesse and our Elector Frederic have maintained musicians, and now the emperor, King Ferdinand and the Duke of Bavaria are doing so. Therefore it is written of David that he maintained both male and female singers.[2]

[1] 1 Sam. xvi, 23.
[2] Ecclesiastes ii, 8.

" Singing is a fine, noble art and exercise. It has nothing to do with the world; it is removed from the contentions of the market and the court. The singer fears no evil; he shuts out all cares and is happy."

At the house of Wolfgang Reissenbusch they sang at table. Luther said: " Music is a noble gift of God, next to theology. I would not change my little knowledge of music for a great deal. Youths should be trained in this art, for it makes fine, clever people."

" That was a very wise regulation of the ancients that required men to exercise themselves, lest they fall into debauchery, excessive drinking and gambling. Therefore, I heartily admire those noble exercises, especially two, music and gymnastic games; of which the former serves to drive away care, the latter to practise the limbs by jumping and wrestling; but the most important reason is that we may not fall into other habits of drink, lust and gaming, as, alas, we see at the courts and in the cities. Then it is only: ' Here's to you! Swill it down!' After that one plays for a hundred florins. So it goes when manly exercises are despised."

" Dear friend, play for me as David played.

I believe that if David were now arisen from
the dead, he would wonder at the progress
that has been made in music. When he
played, it must have been like this: 'My
soul doth magnify the Lord, etc.' "— he
sang at the octave — " for the lute was simply
an instrument of ten strings.[1] How does it
happen that with reference to secular things
we have so many a fine poem and so many
a beautiful song, while for spiritual edification we have such wretched, cold things."

[1] Psalm xcii, 3.

18. ASTRONOMY AND ASTROLOGY.

" Astronomy is the oldest of all the sciences and has contributed to the progress of many arts; it was well known to the ancients, and especially to the Hebrews, who observed most diligently the course of the heavenly bodies, in accordance with God's command to Abraham: ' Look now toward heaven and number the stars.' "[1]

Then Luther spoke concerning the three-fold movement of the heavens: " The first is the primary motion, of great swiftness, which is perhaps caused by an angel; in twenty-four hours the whole firmament is revolved a thousand miles in a jiffy. It is wonderful how quickly the whole sky is thus wheeled around. If the sun and stars were made of iron, silver or gold, they would soon be melted as a result of their enormous velocity. For a star is greater than the earth, and consider how innumerable the stars are. The second movement of the heavens is that of the planets, which take a course peculiar to themselves. The third is a tremulous motion, according to a theory

[1] Gen. xv, 5.

recently set forth, but which is still very doubtful."

"The comet is a star which wanders about like the planets; but it is a bastard among the planets, a proud star which takes possession of the whole sky, as if it were the only one there. It partakes of the character of heretics, who think that they alone are wise and act haughtily toward others."

"I praise astronomy and mathematics, which have to do with demonstrations, and I think that any star is greater than the earth, and that the sun is by far the greatest of the stars; for astrology I have no respect."

"To believe in the stars is idolatry, which is contrary to the first commandment."

"No one will persuade me, neither Paul nor an angel from heaven, nor even Melanchthon, to believe in the predictions of astrology, which are mistaken so many times that nothing is more unreliable. For if they prophesy correctly even two or three times, they make known their prophecies; if they fail, they keep them secret." — Then someone asked: "Doctor, how is this argument to be answered, that since physicians have the power to predict, astrologers have it also?" "Physicians," he replied, "have certain symptoms and experience to guide them, and often hit the truth, although they sometimes fail, but astrologers very frequently fail and are rarely right."

Someone asked: " Doctor, the Scriptures say that God made two great lights and fixed all the stars in the firmament; the astronomers, on the other hand, say that the moon is the least and lowest of the stars. Which shall we believe, the authority of Scripture or the demonstrations of astronomy?" The doctor answered: " From the theory of eclipses, which is supported by accurate demonstrations, we are convinced that astronomical theories ought not to be rejected. I believe, therefore, that Moses spoke according to our power of comprehension, describing the moon as it seems to us; as Vergil speaks of a blazing star, according to the impression it makes and the capacity of the ordinary person to understand. For the Scriptures often give proof of our infirmity."

" I am unable to admire sufficiently the human understanding for having observed with so great accuracy the orbits of the planets. It is very likely that this was an achievement of the patriarchs, as a result of divine suggestion. Afterwards came the soothsayer astrology, which spoiled astronomy."

Speaking of the text: "Let them be for signs,"[1] Luther said: "God meant true signs, as eclipses of the sun and moon, not those uncertain ones;[2] they are a human invention."

Mention was made of a new astronomer[3] who wished to prove that the earth moved and went around, not the sky or the firmament or the sun or the moon. It was just as when one was sitting on a wagon or boat which was moving, it seemed to him that he was standing still and resting, and that the earth and trees moved by. "So it goes," [said Luther], "whoever wants to be clever must not be content with what any one else has done, but must do something of his own and then pretend it was the best ever accomplished. The fool wants to change the whole science of astronomy. But the Holy Scripture clearly shows us that Joshua commanded the sun, not the earth, to stand still."[4]

[1] Gen. i, 14.

[2] Those of the astrologers.

[3] Copernicus, whose epoch-making work *De orbium coelestium revolutionibus* was printed as its author was dying by the Protestant Reformer Osiander at Nuremberg in 1543. He had arrived at his momentous conclusions as early as 1507, and Luther, who is speaking on June 4, 1539, had heard of them from one of his numerous Nuremberg friends.

[4] Joshua, x, 12, 13.

19. THE HUMANISTS.

" Lorenzo Valla is the best Italian[1] whom I have seen or heard of in all my life. His treatise on free will is good. He has sought simplicity both in piety and in style. Erasmus seeks it in style only; piety he ridicules."

" Lorenzo Valla was a good man, pure, simple, clever, and candid. He accomplished more than all the other Italians have ever done. He wished in every way to consult the interests of Italian youth and planned how literature might be promoted. He has written a good book on free will. He has joined piety with letters."

" Dr. Mutian[2] believes there is no God. Desperate with poverty he took poison and so committed suicide. He left after him his book on religion which he dared not publish while alive. Thus also Erasmus wishes to leave his faith behind him, which he dares not confess during life. Such men will not say what they think. They are paltry

[1] The word which Luther uses here for Italian is Walh, a pun on Valla. The equivalent for Walh in modern German is Wälsch.

[2] Conrad Mutianus Rufus (1471 — March 30, 1526), a humanist whose system was nearly allied to pantheism. Luther knew him in 1516. The date of this saying is 1532.

fellows who would measure everything by their own wisdom and think that if God existed he would make another and a better world. But our God will save that for the world to come. This world is only a preparation for that. The scaffold is not taken down until the building is ready. The painter needs brush and paint until he has made his picture. So this world is but a preparation for the other."

" All who pray, curse. Thus when I say, ' Hallowed be thy name,' I curse Erasmus and all who think contrary to the Word."

Luther said that the Elector Frederic had once met Erasmus at Cologne[1] and had given him a damask gown, but afterwards had said to Spalatin: "What sort of a man is he? One never knows where he is." Duke George said: " Plague take him," (for Duke George was a rustic in manners) " one knows not what he is driving at. I prefer the Wittenbergers; they say yes or no." Luther added: " We say it to cheat the pope." Then Severus[2] said of Erasmus: " I knew

[1] On November 5, 1520, for the purpose of asking his opinion of Luther.

[2] Wolfgang Schiefer, who studied at Vienna, 1518, and at Basle, 1521. At the latter place he learned to know Erasmus. In 1522 he went to the Netherlands and in the following year to Wittenberg where he studied two years. Later he became

him and of all pestilent men none was worse
than he. A certain priest told me that he
believed neither in God nor in immortality,[1]
and that he once burst forth into this blasphemy: ' that if God did not exist, he would
like to rule the world with his own wisdom.' "
Then said the doctor:[2] " He arrogates to
himself the divinity he would like to take
from Christ, whom, in his Colloquies, he
compares with Priapus[3] and whom he mocks
in his *Catechism* and especially in his de-
testable *Miscellany*.[4] He despised all others
and compared them with himself, and thought
us who did not understand his ambiguity

tutor to the son of Ferdinand, afterwards Maximilian II.
During the year 1540 he was Luther's guest. Kroker,
Catherina von Bora, p. 180.

[1] No such expression or opinions are found in Erasmus'
works. Charges of atheism were bandied about freely at
this time, for any serious doctrinal disagreement was regarded
as tantamount to it. On Luther's relations with Erasmus,
which were very much strained after 1524, *cf.* Smith, *Luther*,
199f. This saying occurs in 1540.

[2] Luther.

[3] Erasmus did not compare Christ and Priapus, but Luther
considered the close juxtaposition of their names, in Erasmus'
Colloquies, blasphemous.

[4] The *Farrago nova epistolarum*, 1519, to which Luther
refers in a letter of March, 1520, Enders, ii, 369. Luther
probably means *Erasmi Epistolæ ad diversos*, 1521, which he
refers to as the *Farrago*, in a letter of May 15, 1522, Enders,
iii, 360. This reference shows that he was angry at Erasmus
at that time, but no letter of Luther challenging him to fight
is extant. The letter of April, 1524 (Enders, iv, 319) was
written with just the opposite purpose.

silly, infatuated little geese and dolls. In my letter which displeased Philip I challenged him but he would, not fight. For I had some things from his *Miscellany* with which I wished to charge him."

Melanchthon repeated a saying of Erasmus as follows: "After the theologians invented the Father and the Son, they added the Holy Ghost also, that they might have a pretty number."[1]

"Erasmus of Rotterdam," said Luther, "thinks that the Christian religion is either a comedy or a tragedy, and that the things therein described never actually happened, but were invented for the purpose of moral training."

As Luther examined a likeness of Erasmus, he said: "The expression of his face indicates shrewdness, but he only scoffs at God and religion. He uses, to be sure, the greatest words, 'Holy Christ, the holy Word, the holy sacraments,' but in truth he is very indifferent to these things. He has a gift for biting satire, and his writing is very clever, as in his *Praise of Folly* and his *Julius*;[2]

[1] *Bellum numerum.* Compare the German proverb: All good things are in threes.

[2] On the authorship of this work see Smith's *Luther's Correspondence*, p. 63. It is there held to be correctly ascribed to Erasmus.

but in teaching he is very cold. He can prate indeed, but his eloquence is made, not born. When he prepares a sermon, it sounds like an artificially constructed thing, utterly cold. As Cicero says, ' there is no better way to convince others than first to convince oneself.' "

" To Erasmus it seems ridiculous that God should be born of a poor maid. Lucian has laughed at all the gods, but Erasmus is a greater knave than he. But at the last day he will feel differently, and [seeing us among the saved] will say: ' I thought the life of those people was foolish.' "

" Erasmus is bad through and through, as is evident in all his books, especially his *Colloquies*. He says: ' I do not speak; the speaking is done by the characters who are introduced.' If I were well I would have it out with him. To him ' Father, Son and Holy Ghost ' is a ridiculous thing. God allows us to play with apples, pears and nuts, and to jest with our wives, but to do that with God and his majesty is not allowed."

" Erasmus is worthy of great hatred. I warn you all to regard him as God's enemy. He inflames the baser passions of young boys and regards Christ as I regard Klaus Narr.[1]

[1] The court fool of the Ernestine princes.

He teaches adults nothing. Our solace is
faith in Christ. We have often died for it;
let us hold fast to it alone. I will remain
true to Christ, and am willing to die for him.
I have been baptized in him; I can do
nothing and I know nothing, except what he
has taught me."

" I wonder that a man can fall so far from
the knowledge of God as Erasmus has fallen. He is as certain that there is no God
and no eternal life, as I am certain that I see.
Lucian is not so certain of it as is Erasmus."

" Erasmus wrote against me [a book called]
Hyperaspistes. But as there lives a God in
heaven, he will perceive sometime what he
has done."

" That thought of Erasmus is the greatest
and most dangerous of all temptations,
namely, that God is unjust when the righteous suffer misfortune while the unrighteous
prosper; for if God were just and adminis-
tered human affairs justly, the good would not
fare ill nor the bad well. This opinion concerning God is plainly Epicurean and impious, and arises from the fact that they who
hold it regard the nature of man as unim-
paired, while on the contrary our judgment,
reason and intellect have been corrupted and
made defective by original sin. Therefore

they think God to be such a being as he
seems to them and their faulty eyes. They
have blue spectacles on and through them
they see God discolored, like everything
else, nor are they able to see him otherwise.
For they do not see how much evil original
sin has brought us, nor how it has corrupted
our judgment. From reason they conclude
that original sin is lust, putting it in the flesh
only and in a certain base animal function,
namely, the reproductive. And so all writers
speak of carnal concupiscence as original sin,
ignoring infidelity and pride of heart, and
esteeming these as nothing."

"With Erasmus it is translation and
nothing else. He is never in earnest; he
is ambiguous and a caviller. In his New
Testament he brings in all the Fathers:
'Thus says Ambrosius'; 'Thus says Augustine.' Why? That he may disturb the
reader and make him think that the doctrine
is very uncertain. He abuses all of us
Christians without discrimination, not ex-
cepting Paul nor any other of the pious.
Master Philip told me that Erasmus said on
one occasion that he wished to overthrow the
foundations of our doctrine; and this he is
trying exceedingly hard to accomplish in all
his writings. Philip has one of his dialogues

entitled *Lucian Concerning Christ*,[1] which is said to contain gross blasphemies."

Speaking of Erasmus' edition of the New Testament Luther said: " I wish that it might be suppressed because of its Epicureanism[2] and the many false doctrines which have been inserted. He has destroyed many, body and soul. He is one cause of the Sacramentarians. He has injured the Gospel as much as he has advanced the science of grammar. He has been a shameless fellow. Zwingli was led astray by him; he won over Egranus[3] also, who has about as much faith as he himself. He died without the cross and without light. If I were a young man, I would study the Greek tongue till I knew it perfectly, and then bring out another edition " [*sc.* of the New Testament].

" It is the opinion of the pope and all the cardinals, and even of Erasmus, that religion is all a fable, but that it should be preserved in order that the royal power and the papal monarchy may be maintained;

[1] Erasmus translated various dialogues of Lucian, but none is extant with this title, nor is there any dialogue of Lucian with this title, though the Greek satirist occasionally alludes to the Founder of Christianity.

[2] *I.e.*, skepticism.

[3] John Sylvius Egranus (John Wildenauer of Eger) was a preacher in Zwickau and afterwards in Joachimsthal. He died in 1535.

these institutions, they think, would collapse without the fear of religion, and it would also be impossible to hold the common people to their tasks. For this purpose they make use of religion, in the truth of which they do not believe."

" Egranus was a proud ass, and what he said about not exalting Christ too high, he had learned from Erasmus. After he had visited him, nothing that he had formerly praised, pleased him any more."

20. HUMAN REASON AND THE PHILOSOPHY OF THE PAGANS.

" Erasmus, Oecolampadius, Zwingli and Carlstadt wish to measure everything by their own wisdom, and so are confounded. I, however, thank God that I know and believe that God is much wiser than I am. He can do things that are quite beyond my comprehension; he is able to make invisible things visible, for all these things which are now being accomplished by the light of the Gospel are invisible things made visible. Who would have hoped ten years ago that things would ever be as they are now? But the flesh is most wicked."

" God promises us forgiveness of sins through grace and also adds threats of punishment: 'Unless ye believe, ye will perish.'[1] Before we would believe that and accept pardon freely offered, we would rather torture ourselves to death, or walk in heavy armor to the shrine of St. James.[2] In short, to the world belong not truth and life, but

[1] Mark xvi, 16.

[2] At Santiago de Compostella in Spain, a chief resort of pilgrims during the Middle Ages. The cathedral is said to contain the sepulchre and relics of the apostle St. James.

falsehood and slaughter, of which the one is the pope, the other the Turk."

" Those who made Fortune a goddess were wise men: they saw that what happens in the world is not governed by human reason, nor sustained by human strength, but by divine."

Luther was asked whether the light of reason was useful to the theologian. He replied: " I make this distinction: Reason corrupted by the devil is harmful, and the cleverer and more richly endowed it is, the more harm it does, as we see in wise men who are led by their reason to reject the Word; but reason informed by the Spirit is a help in interpreting the Holy Scriptures. Thus the tongue of Cochlaeus[1] speaks blasphemies, while my tongue speaks the praise of God, and nevertheless it is the same instrument in each case; it is a tongue before faith and after faith, and while simply as a tongue it does not help one's faith, it does so when the mind is illumined by the Spirit. So reason also is of service to faith, when it is enlightened, since it reflects upon things; but without faith it is of no use, just as the tongue of the unbeliever

[1] John Dobneck, commonly called Cochlaeus (1479–1552), a prominent Catholic opponent of the Reformer.

speaks idle blasphemies, as we see in Duke George. When, however, reason is enlightened by the Spirit, it takes all its thoughts from the Word; then substance remains, while vanity disappears."

"No error is so gross, that it may not appear most plausible, if you consider it with the reason alone without the aid of the Word, as, for example, the error of the Manichaeans[1] concerning the two principles of good and evil; for, looking about over the world, they saw in everything some good and some evil. Now the reason that they fell into such a stupid error was that they did not consider the first article of the creed, or considered it only carelessly, otherwise they would not have admitted another God. For thus it stands in the creed: 'I believe in one God.' Origen also discusses the existence of evil, whether God is the author of it. We hold, however, that he is not really the author of evil, but that he permits it to exist, according to the text: 'So I gave them up unto their own hearts' lust.' "[2]

"Philosophy ought to be content to investigate matter, its primary and secondary qualities, and to distinguish accidents

---

[1] A sect of heretics, who derived from Persia their doctrine of dualism.
[2] Ps. lxxxi, 12.

from the substance. Concerning causes it is unable to reach any certainty. For a chicken just hatched from the shell retains its peculiar nature, and nothing is added by a second cause. How can the stars affect a boy so as to make of him a man, and how can philosophy speak correctly of causes, since it does not[1] presuppose the existence of either God or the devil, and yet one is called the creator and the other the prince of the world. Therefore its speculations are of slight account."

Luther said: " Alas! We are indeed poor people! We should be contemptible paupers if things were to remain as they are forever." Someone then remarked: " The heathen argue that since the good suffer ills here, there must be another life." " Yes," replied the doctor, " that is the best argument, and all the heathen have it. Less important is the argument of Plato[2] that the soul does not consist of elements, and his proof: ' Because ideas and such swift movements are not of the nature of an element,' is of no value, although Augustine discourses

[1] The negative is not present in the text as given by Kroker, *Luthers Tischreden*, p. 205, but it seems necessary to supply it. The haste with which the students were obliged to write, makes the text of the table talk faulty.

[2] In his dialogue, Phaedo, and also in the Phaedrus.

about it vigorously, and has made many inductions; for even a sheep takes on swift motions when it sees a wolf! Therefore their arguments do not help us; but they suggest to us that we should think of the creator."

"Aristotle is certainly an Epicurean.[1] He does not believe that God presides over human affairs, or if he does, he thinks that God governs the world much as a sleepy maid rocks the baby. But Cicero got much further. I believe that he gathered together whatever of good he found in all the Greek writers. He proves the existence of God from the generation of species, a very strong argument, which has often moved me: a cow always bears a cow, a horse a horse; a cow never bears a horse, nor a horse a cow, nor a goldfinch a siskin. It follows therefore that there must be some power which regulates all this. We have very obvious proof that God exists, in the exact and perpetual movement of the heavenly bodies: we find that the sun rises and sets from year to year in its regular place. We reach the same conclusion from the certainty with which at the appointed time the seasons succeed each other. But those things, which are a part of our daily

[1] As used by Luther this word always means skeptic.

[118]

experience, do not excite our wonder, they are hardly deemed worthy of notice. But if a person should be educated from his youth up in a dark place, and after twenty years released, he would be astonished at the sun and wonder what it was and why it always took a certain course at any given time! But to us it is nothing, because it is so common."

" Human nature must be far, far, far above brute nature, for however strong and wild a beast may be, it must stand in awe of man and think of the text: ' Have dominion over them.'[1] That a man should live like a pig does not agree with his nature and position as a governor. The brutes are only concerned with things natural and not with what is achieved by labor. But we are commanded to do something and be a part of the state and family and to rule. Do not be lazy men fit only to eat what others gather. Cicero has a fine argument from the conservation of species. An apple-tree does not bear pears, nor a cow an ass, there-fore the world must be ruled by divine providence. Let genera and species re-joice, as Aristotle says, against the alche-mists. For no one can change this: oxen

[1] Gen. i, 28.

remain oxen and men men. Had I lived
at the time of Epicurus and been a bad
fellow, I should have liked to play him a
knavish trick, taking his wife and daughter
and bringing them to shame, and then I
would have said to him: 'O, there is no
divine providence! God doesn't attend to
those things, look out for yourself!' Cicero
was a fine philosopher who wrote much and
easily. He will sit higher [in the next world]
than Duke George, or Margrave Joachim I
of Brandenburg, who died between two
courtesans. If they were as well off as
Cicero is, they would be happy!"

"Cicero is much more learned than
Aristotle, and his style is clear. He has
taught philosophy well, and his *Offices* is a
charming book! If I were young I would
devote myself to Cicero, after my opinions
however had been thoroughly established by
a study of sacred literature."

"Philosophy has no knowledge of sacred
things, and I am anxious lest it get mixed
up too much with theology. This practice
I do not disapprove, but we should understand that philosophy is merely a shadow, a
comedy, and a 'certain civil righteousness!'[1]

[1] This phrase is used in the Augsburg Confession of natural
as opposed to religious virtue.

But to regard it as the essence of theology, that won't do. Neither do I think that faith should be called an accident or quality. For these are philosophical terms indicating that faith inheres in us as color in a wall. But faith in the mind is a different thing, for it is a substance; but yet it is not material in the sense in which the body is material."

" If one consults reason alone, he is unable to assent to the articles of our faith. The Turk keeps his subjects to their work more by the influence of religion than by force of arms, for he believes that God is the all-powerful creator of heaven and earth, that Christ is his prophet, that by faithful service to the state we are able to merit heaven, etc. But I have learned, apart from Scripture, amidst the greatest agony and temptation, that Christ is God and that he became flesh, and in like manner I have learned the truth of the article concerning the Trinity. Wherefore it is not so much that I believe these articles, as that I know by experience that they are true. For in the greatest temptations nothing is able to help us, except our belief that the Son of God became flesh and bone, and sits on the right hand of the Father and intercedes for us. There is no more powerful consolation than this. And God has defended this article from the beginning of the world against all heretics, who are innumerable, and he defends it today against the Turk and the pope, and he is always proving it by miracles, and he brings it about that we call his Son the Son of God and the true God, and he hears all of us who call upon him in Christ's name. For what has preserved us until today in so great perils, but prayer to Christ? Whoever says that it was Master Philip and I and others, lies about us. God does it for the sake of Christ, of whom today the apostles preach: ' He whom you hanged seven weeks ago still lives! '[1] If it were not for the blindness of the human heart, by this time all would have become believers! Therefore we shall hold to those articles even against reason. They have stood and they will stand.''

Some say that the soul after it takes flight from the mortal body migrates to heaven, as Christ said: " Today shalt thou be with me in paradise." To this Luther replied: " Yes, but what is meant by *today?* It is true that souls hear, perceive, and see after death; but how it is done, we do not understand. Where then do they remain, that

[1] Acts ii, 23f.

hang upon the gallows? If we undertake to gave an account of such things after the manner of this life, then we are fools. Christ has given a good answer; for his disciples also were without doubt just as curious. 'He that believeth in me, though he were dead, yet shall he live ';[1] likewise: 'Whether we live, or whether we die, we are the Lord's.'[2] " Before this he had said to his wife, Katie: "Yes, you are already in heaven! Christians look forward to the resurrection of the dead, and the dead are living. For instance, Abraham lives. God is God of the living. If now one would say; 'The soul of Abraham lives with God, his body lies here dead,' it would be a distinction which to my mind is mere rot! I will dispute it. One must say: 'The whole Abraham, the entire man, lives!' But you tear away a piece of Abraham and say: 'That lives.' Thus the philosophers talk: 'After the soul has migrated from this home etc.' It must be a foolish soul, if it were in heaven, to have a desire for the body! "

When some one had said that there was a similar dispute concerning the location of the infernal regions, since no definite place had been set aside for evil spirits, he added:

[1] John, xi, 25.   [2] Rom. xiv, 8.

" Scripture tells us that; Peter says in the second epistle, chapter ii, that they are in chains. They do not suffer their punishment yet, although they have been judged. For if they already had their punishment, the devils would not be doing so much wickedness."

Then some one remarked: " And nevertheless the creed says: ' He descended into hell.' " Luther replied: " That is something to be believed! We cannot understand it. So it goes. People will dispute how trinity exists in unity; since there is no relation between the finite and the infinite, how nature can produce that monster without form, the God-man, etc. They will pay no heed to the article concerning justification. If only we devoted this time to studying how we ought to believe and pray and be pious! But since we understand that [we are not contented], but must dispute about something higher, that we can never understand, and moreover our Lord God wills that we shall not understand it. Such is human nature! It wills to do what it is prevented from doing; the other it leaves without and comes then to the Wherefore, Wherefore, Wherefore? So it goes, when philosophy gets into theology. When the devil came to Eve with the Wherefore, the game was up. Therefore, one should take care! As a safeguard, get down on the knees a while and pray for a time a Paternoster! It is much more useful to you. O, dear Lord God, protect us from the devil and also from ourselves!"

21. JUSTIFICATION.

" It is the opinion of Augustine that the law fulfilled by the strength of reason does not justify, as good works do not justify the heathen; but if the Holy Spirit should be present to aid, then the works of the law justify. But it is not the question whether the law or the works of reason justify, but whether the law fulfilled in the Spirit justifies. I reply that it does not, and that one who fulfils the law in every respect by virtue of the Holy Spirit, must nevertheless implore the mercy of God, who has determined that we shall be saved not through the law, but through Christ. Works never bring peace to the conscience, and Christ never would have been depressed in spirit, had he not been weighed down by the law, to which for our sake he subjected himself."

" No one is able to write or say anything fitting concerning grace, unless he has been greatly tried by spiritual temptations. Monks and lawyers are unable to discuss it properly."

" If I dispute with Satan concerning the law, the victory is his. Therefore I will help stone Moses, lest he remain with the contumacious rather than with the timid and conscientious."

" The wicked are made worse by the preaching of the gospel; for they learn from it only the license of the flesh. Therefore the common people should have the law, not the gospel. They are like ill-mannered, rowdyish boys, who are only made worse by being honored instead of flogged. Bad children need the rod, not sweets."

" If Christ comes to you when you are sorrowful on account of your sins and speaks as Moses, saying, ' What have you done? ' then strike him dead. If, however, he speaks with you as your God and Saviour, then prick up both ears."

" God demands nothing else from those who believe in him than: ' This do in remembrance of me.'[1] If you say however: ' Yes, Lord, but I shall get slapped in the face for it,' he will answer you: ' Call upon me in the day of trouble and I will deliver thee,'[2] and that is a service to God that is easily rendered. Likewise it is easy to obey the command: ' Seek ye first the kingdom of heaven, and then be of good cheer, for all things will be added unto you.'[3] He promised

[1] Luke, xxii, 19.   [2] Ps. xci, 15.   [3] Math. vi, 33.

us help even on the cross; what therefore can we lack?"

"That life, grace and salvation may not be earned by good works is plain, because works are not spiritual birth, but the fruit of that birth; for we do not become sons and heirs of God, justified and sanctified Christians, by means of works, but having been made, born and created such, we do the works. Thus life, salvation and grace necessarily precede works, just as a tree does not become a meritorious tree by reason of its fruit, but having been born a tree, it bears fruit. For we are born and created just by the word of grace; we are not fashioned, prepared and made just by the voice of the law or of works. Works earn something other than life, grace and salvation, namely: certain special things such as praise, glory and favor; just as a tree deserves to be loved, cultivated, praised and honored by the others on account of its fruit. Look to the [spiritual] birth and status of a Christian and at once you have destroyed [the need for] the merits of works to win grace and salvation from sin, death and the devil. Infants are saved by faith alone without works, therefore faith alone justifies. If the power of God can accomplish this in one case it can in all, for it is not effected by the power

of the infant but by the power of faith;
nor does the impotence of the child accomplish it, otherwise that impotence would be
merit in itself, or equivalent to merit.
We should like to boast to the Lord of our
works; we should like to gain salvation
through them. But he will not permit us to
do so. Conscience tells me that I am not
justified by works, but no one believes it.
'That thou mightest be justified when thou
speakest; against thee only have I sinned;
in thy sight have I done evil.'[1] What is the
meaning of the words: 'Forgive us our
debts'? I will not be righteous. What
could be easier than to say: 'I am a sinful
man; thou, God, art just'? That would be
extremely simple. But we torture ourselves,
for the Spirit says: 'Thou art just,' and the
flesh is unable to add: 'That thou mightest
be justified when thou speakest.'"

Speaking of the words of Paul[2] — "For
I am not ashamed of the gospel of Christ:
for it is the power of God unto salvation, to
every one that believeth; to the Jew first,
and also to the Greek. For therein is the
righteousness of God revealed from faith
to faith: as it is written, The just shall live
by faith," — Luther said: "These words

[1] Ps. li, 4.   [2] Romans, i, 16f.

were ever running in my mind. For I
had not been able to understand the phrase
' the righteousness of God,'[1] wherever it
stands in Scripture, otherwise than that God
was both righteous himself and judged right-
eously. Sometimes I would ply myself too
warmly with this text. I stood and knocked[2]
if haply there might be some one to open
unto me, but there was no one to open.
I did not know at all what it meant until I
came in my reading to the words: ' The just
shall live by his faith.'[3] This sentence is an
explanation of that ' righteousness of God.'
When I discovered this I was filled with a
joy passing all others. And thus the road

[1] *Justitia Dei.* This saying is one of many giving Luther's
account of his conversion, of which the most famous was
published in the preface to his works, 1545 (reprinted, *Lutheri
opera latina varii argumenti,* Erlangen, 1865, i, 15ff). The
present saying is two or three years earlier. According to
Luther the crux with him was the phrase "justitia Dei,"
which at first he understood as the justice of God judging men;
later, apparently in 1515, he came to see that it was "the
righteousness of God" in us, which, being apprehended by
faith, was the cause of man's salvation rather than of his
reprobation. On the subject of Luther's conversion see
American Journal of Psychology, xxiv, 360ff (1913) and
Harvard Theological Review, vi, 407ff (1913). The most
brilliant explanation of the phenomena of the religious life
in general is found in A. R. Burr's *Religious Confessions and
Confessants,* 1914. *Cf.* especially p. 173, for light on the
present subject.

[2] Matthew, vii, 7.

[3] Romans, i, 17. Luther began lecturing on Romans in
May, 1515.

was opened to me when I read in Psalms:[1] 'In thy justice make me free,' that is, 'In thy mercy make me free.' Prior to that time I dreaded and hated the Psalms and other parts of Scripture whenever they mentioned 'the righteousness of God,' by which I understood that he himself was righteous and judged us according to our sins, not that he accepted us and made us righteous. All Scripture stood as a wall, until I was enlightened by the words: 'The just shall live by faith.' From this I learned that the righteousness of God is faith in the mercy of God, by which he himself justifies us through grace."

Explaining the meaning of justification through faith by a comparison, Luther said: " A son is not made heir to his father's estate, but he is born an heir and even succeeds to it without any work or merit, but in the meantime, nevertheless, the father commands and urges his son to apply himself diligently to this or that, and promises him some little gift as a reward, that he may obey more

---

[1] There is no verse in Psalms just like this. Luther was thinking of Psalm iv, 2, 3, as is shown by his commentary based on lectures delivered in the winter of 1513–1514. In this he says: "My righteousness is not mine but his who has heard me. . . For in that he pities me, *ipso facto* he justifies me. His mercy is my righteousness." *Werke*, Weimar, iii, 42f.

willingly. He says for example: ' If you are good and obedient, and study faithfully, I will buy you a new coat,' or, ' Come here to me, I will give you a fine apple.' Thus he trains the son to habits of industry; although the inheritance belongs to him for other reasons, yet these things are done for his education. Even so God deals with us. He coaxes us with promises of spiritual and temporal blessings, although eternal life is freely given to those who believe in Christ, whom he regards as his adopted children. Thus we ought to teach in the church that God will reward good works, but we should keep none the less pure the article of justification, which is the head and cause of all other promises. Ought we to say then: ' Believe, and you will be saved, no matter what you do'? No, that is nonsense. Let us remember, therefore, that it is to guide us in the right path that God makes those promises of reward by which he invites and entices us to do well, to serve our neighbor and to be obedient."

Luther said many things concerning the majesty of the article of justification, which is a matter not comprehended by human wisdom; for we are all by nature more zealous for righteousness than for the free mercy of

God. Therefore the parable in Matthew xx concerning the laborers in the vineyard is the most destructive of thunderbolts against the opinion of the flesh. He also related the anecdote from the lives of the fathers concerning a certain anchorite of most holy life, who was in the agony of death: "When another old father, together with a young man, wished to visit him in his cell, these two were met by a robber, who was also going to see the sick monk. The robber, standing before the door, where he saw and heard the piety of the dying man, breathed a sigh, saying: 'Alas, I also should have lived thus!' The sick man replied: 'Certainly, thou shouldst have lived a just life, as I have done, hadst thou wished to be saved,' and with these words he expired. The young man saw his soul being borne away by devils, and he wept. [As the old man and the youth departed], the robber, who repented his sins, followed them, wishing to confess and to obtain absolution, and he came with such haste that he fell headlong and died; and as he died angels received his soul, seeing which the youth laughed. When the old man observed the strange conduct of his companion, who wept at the death of a most saintly man and laughed at the misfortune of the robber [he asked the reason]. The youth replied that he had acted piously in weeping when he saw the devils carry off the spirit of the proud man, while here he had witnessed the salvation of a penitent soul and had rightly rejoiced. So it goes in the kingdom of Christ, where the last shall be first;[1] for God can endure no sin less patiently than the proud arrogance of the self-righteous."

"Augustine did not rightly understand the doctrine of justification by faith."[2]

[1] Matt. xix, 30.

[2] This saying is particularly interesting in view of the opinion sometimes held that Luther derived his doctrine from this father of the church.

22. PREDESTINATION.

Luther said: "When a man begins to discuss predestination, the temptation is like an inextinguishable fire; the more he disputes, the more he despairs. Our Lord God is opposed to this disputation and accordingly he has provided against it baptism, the Word, the sacraments, and various signs. In these we should trust and say: 'I am baptized, I believe in Jesus Christ; what does it concern me, whether or not I am predestined?' He has given us ground to stand on, that is, Jesus Christ, and through him we may climb to heaven. He is the one way and the gate to the Father. But when we begin in the devil's name to build first on the roof above, scorning the ground, then we fall! If we only could believe in the promises which God has given, and direct our gaze on God himself as he speaks, we should esteem his words highly; but when we hear them from the mouth of a poor human being, we pay no more heed than to the lowing of a cow."

"The discussion of predestination should be wholly avoided. Staupitz used to say: 'If you have a desire to dispute concerning

[135]

predestination, begin with the wounds of
Christ, and the desire will cease; if you
continue to argue about it, you will lose
Christ, the Word, the sacraments and everything.' I forget all that Christ and God are,
when I get to thinking about this matter,
and come to believe that God is a villain.
We ought to remain by the Word, in which
God is revealed to us and salvation offered,
if we believe it. Moreover in trying to
understand predestination, we forget God,
we cease to praise and begin to blaspheme.
In Christ, however, are hid all treasures;
without him none may be had. Therefore
we should give no place whatever to this
argument concerning predestination."

"I have been vexed," said the doctor,
"with speculations as to what God is going
to do with me, but at length I rejected these
thoughts, and threw myself on God's will as
revealed in the Scriptures. We can do no
more. The hidden will cannot be investi-
gated by man, and God conceals it on account of that extremely shrewd spirit, the
devil, in order that he may fail. The revealed will the devil has learned from us;
the hidden will God keeps to himself. We
can learn enough from the humanity of
Christ, in which the Father has revealed

himself, and we are foolish to neglect the Word and will of the Father as revealed in Christ, while we scrutinize mysteries which ought to be adored. On account of this many come to grief."

23. THE PAPACY.

"The world is unwilling to accept God as the true God, and the devil as the real devil, therefore it is compelled to endure their representative, namely the pope, who is the false vicar of God and the true vicar of the devil."

"The papacy is a government by which the wicked and those who despise God deserve to be ruled, for it is fitting that those who are unwilling to obey God of their own accord should be forced to obey a scoundrel."

"The pope is truly a devil, next to the real devil himself. This is easily proved in this Clement,[1] for he is bad because he is an Italian, worse for being a Florentine, and worst because he is a bastard. If you can think of anything worse, add it."

"The pope is devising most wicked plots, but he will have no more success than did Ferdinand,[2] the king of Hungary. After Satan there is no worse rogue than the pope. He has riches, power and authority; but the

[1] Pope Clement VII, 1523–1534. *Cf.* Smith, *Luther*, p. 236. Luther speaks in 1531.

[2] The bigoted Catholic brother of Charles V, who was at this time acting against the Lutherans at the Diet of Ratisbon, 1532.

Lord's prayer is sufficient protection against him. He has seen Rome submerged,[1] plundered and desolated,[2] and nevertheless this good Clement is wholly unmoved by these warnings. He must indeed be a fine fellow, who is frightened by no terrors and devises evils without end! And if the king of France, with whom he is in alliance, is defeated by the emperor, he will invite in the Turk as our guest. But his schemes will fail. He is a Florentine, a bastard, and an enemy of God."

"The pope put me under the ban, and since then I have grown larger in body and soul; now I put him under the ban, but my ban is stronger than his, for he is growing smaller and weaker, and will yet be wholly ruined."

"The people of Rome used to say that since the time of Peter no pope had been more powerful than Julius[3] and now he lies in the dust. Alas, priests should preach and pray."

"One time when two persons were disputing at the pope's table as to the immortality

---

[1] By the flood of Oct. 8 and 9, 1530. See Cellini, *Autobiography*, Bk. i, chap. 55, also *Luther's Briefwechsel*, ed. Enders, viii, 325f.

[2] In the sack of Rome, 1527.

[3] Julius II, 1503–1513.

of the soul, one being for and the other against the doctrine, the pope finally expressed his opinion, saying that he who held the soul to be immortal had the better of the argument, but that for his part he agreed with the other, for thus he could live more merrily. What a shame that such wretches and Epicureans should have the government of Christian churches! Thus under Leo X it was decreed at the Lateran Council that the priests should wear long coats reaching to the ankles, high shoes, large tonsures, and should not discuss the question whether the soul was mortal or immortal."[1]

When mention was made of the pope and of Rome, and that there were learned men there, Luther said that a certain monk at Rome had preached as follows: " In the time of the martyrs there was *conscientia* (conscience); afterwards in the time of the popes and bishops the syllable *con* was

[1] The editor of the *Tischreden* in the Weimar edition, vol. ii, no. 2213b, referring only to Hefele-Hergenröther's *Konciliengeschichte*, was unable to say whether these statements of Luther were correct or not. An examination of the decrees of this council shows that they are substantially so. In a decree of December 19, 1513, the council condemned the heresy, stated to be rapidly growing, that the soul is mortal, and, in order to remove all ground for error, forbade all the clergy, secular and regular, to lecture for five years at the universities on philosophy or on the classics (poesis). Mansi, *Collectio amplissima conciliorum*, xxxii, 842f. The other regulations spoken of by Luther are found *ibid*. coll. 879ff.

erased from the word, leaving *scientia* (knowledge); now the syllable *sci* has been omitted, and only *entia* (substance or wealth) remains."

"The papacy is doubly founded on the mass, which they call the worship of God and which they make an instrument for raking in all the wealth of the world to give it to the pope. The mass is the rock on which the papists build in spirit and in flesh; it is now fallen in spirit and God will soon destroy it in the flesh. If God lets me die a natural death, he will do a great spite to the papists who would have burned me, and he will set them at nought."

"I believe, thank God! that many papists will be saved, although they never heard the gospel preached as it now is. I mean those to whom the crucifix was shown while they were dying and were told to put all their trust in him who saved them. But it is up with those to whom the monks came with their cowls and self-appointed, supererogatory works."

"The pope has been the greatest money-getter. Emperors and kings coin money from gold and silver, but the pope coins money from all that he has made, from indulgences, the sacraments, dispensations from fasting, by his power both civil and ecclesiastical and by his regulation of marriage. From baptism alone he could get nothing, for infants are born naked and poor and therefore have nothing to give."

On December 12 (1536), Dr. Bugenhagen brought Martin Luther a book[1] on the Council of Constance, telling how it held its sessions and everything it did. That evening Martin Luther read it with continuous attention, and found in it among other things the decree that a safe-conduct to a heretic was not to be observed.[2] Then our father Luther said: "If we are cited and appear,[3] it will be wise to assail them at our first meeting. It is all one whether our wrath comes first or last. Therefore let us attack the papacy with the article of justification: I believe in Jesus Christ; the just shall live by his faith.[4] This thunderbolt would shatter the whole papacy, with its private masses, justifying works, purgatory, monastic life, invocation of the saints

[1] The book was, Ulrich von Richenthal: *Das Concilium, so zu Constantz gehalten ist worden.* 2d edition, Augsburg, December, 1536.

[2] This decree, passed by the council at its XIXth Session, September 23, 1415, is reprinted in Mansi, *Collectio conciliorum,* xxvii, 799, and in Carl Mirbt: *Quellen zur Geschichte des Papsttums,*[3] 1911, no. 319.

[3] *I.e.,* at the council summoned to meet at Mantua in 1537. On this see Smith, *Life and Letters of Luther,* chap. xxviii.

[4] Romans, i, 17.

and pilgrimages. If we stand fast in that, all other articles conceded by us will accomplish nothing. For Campeggio[1] said that before he would let the mass be taken from him, he would let himself be broken on the wheel. I answered that before I would defend that mass, I would let myself be burned to ashes, and more. If we go on in this manner at a council it will soon come to an end, for the two heads, Christ and the devil, must oppose each other, and can never be reconciled. Therefore, no union is to be hoped for from this council, for they come to it, not to yield to Christ, but rashly to judge and condemn."

"Great and insolent has been the avarice of the pope, for the devil has chosen Rome especially as the place of avarice. Thus the ancients said: 'Roma, Radix Omnium Malorum Avaritia.'[2] And in a very old book I found this verse, 'Versus amor mundi caput est et bestia terrae.'[3] For their rapacity is horrible, inasmuch as they wish to seize everything without labor of their hands, without preaching or ministering to

[1] Cardinal Lorenzo Campeggio,† 1539, one of the papal nuncios to negotiate with the Lutherans.

[2] An acrostic meaning, "The root of all evils is avarice."

[3] A rebus meaning, "Amor [love] turned around [i.e., Roma] is the capital of the world and the beast of the earth."

the church, but only by superstition and the sale of their works. Thus Peter paints their greed in excellent words, 'Having their heart full of avarice.'[1] I believe that no one can know what the passion of greed is unless they know Rome, for all other fraud, imposture and greed are nothing compared to the superstition of Rome. Thus at the Diet of Worms[2] the whole empire petitioned the emperor against their rapacity, saying that if he didn't stop it, they would. At that time I had just published in my book to the German nobility what I had found out from Dr. Wick.[3] Then the course of the gospel began excellently, but those three sects, of Carlstadt, Münzer and the Anabaptists, greatly impeded it.[4] But even after that God helped us and brought down the papacy without my wish. Truly great is the power of the pope over kings and rulers, but I attacked it in my book against

[1] 2 Peter ii, 3.

[2] At the Diet of Worms in 1521 a list of grievances, the Gravamina, against ecclesiastical abuses, was drawn up.

[3] Luther's famous pamphlet, *To the Christian Nobility of the German Nation*, exposed many abuses of the papal government at Rome, which he had learned to know through a Dr. John von Wick. Cf. *Luther's Correspondence, translated and edited by Preserved Smith*, vol. i (1913), p. 341.

[4] On this see Smith: *Life and Letters of Martin Luther*, chap. XIII.

excommunication,[1] which book I wrote with no animus against the papacy, but only against the abuse of its power. But they were horrified because their consciences were guilty."

"The papal church has two pillars, the mass and the celibacy of the clergy. From the mass has flowed every kind of impiety, and it has been the most abominable of abominations. And nevertheless they regard it as the highest worship of God. From the earliest years I have been sorely tried as follows: 'If the mass is the highest worship of God, good heavens, how wicked you have been towards God!' But it is certain that the mass is Mauzzim.[2] As to the celibacy of the priesthood, they see themselves that all have concubines! Wherefore I wonder why they are so blind. Marriage is a creation of God, by God ordained. We could not have been deprived of it without our nature's being impaired, and the Gentiles compelled many to enter matrimony. Even as it is we have been reluctant to marry on account of the burden of matrimony,

[1] *Sermon on the Ban*, published 1520.

[2] A Hebrew word interpreted by Luther as the name of a false god. See Daniel xi, 38 (in the German Bible, xii, 3). "Und seiner Väter Gott wird er nicht achten. . . . Aber an dess Statt wird er seinen Gott Maussim ehren."

and nevertheless the papists forbid it. They won't be able to leave it thus. The cloisters of begging friars and all that sort of thing fail of themselves, yet they still seek to defend them. The emperor knows it, but what will he do? His hands are tied."

"No one dared to read the canon law, unless he was anointed, and nevertheless it has neither erudition nor any peculiar merit, nor is it good Latin. I believe that some ignorant monk wrote it. But so sacred was it, that he who opposed it, was thought to move heaven and earth. When I first wrote against the mass and the canon law, I could not believe that any one would be able to yield obedience to me; and I wrote for myself and Staupitz and Wenzel Link. But when the little book[1] appeared, then I found many, who had had my trouble, who were grateful to be freed from so great fear. For under the papacy I saw many, who spoke the words of consecration with such great fear, that they trembled and stammered, although it was a sin to falter in a single syllable. The canons were glad to hear that the mass had been attacked. Ah, how the devil would have laughed in his fist, if we

[1] The sermon on the New Testament, that is, on the Holy Mass, translated in *The Works of Martin Luther*, Philadelphia, 1915, vol. 1, pp. 287ff.

also had suffered martyrdom! No one to-day realizes how miserable we were under the papacy."

"The papists have gained no knowledge of Christ either of the gospel or of faith, so excluded has Christ been from the world. The Turk commands in the east, the pope in the west. These are the last, most perilous times. The papists thought that Christ was a judge, that the gospel was a new law, that faith was an assent or condition agreed to without fear. Thus Eck thinks that faith is an inherent quality of the heart, as color in the wall; that love is the light by which faith may be seen. Such is their philosophy! Since therefore the pope knows nothing else concerning our religion, yet condemns us, we shall not admit the papal legates to the conference at Worms.[1] For that was the agreement. Since the pope is a heretic, an idolater, Antichrist and the red whore reeking with the blood of the pious, therefore we will not admit him to our presence. As a private individual he may listen to our discussion, but he is not to interfere. Even if they are willing to grant us sacerdotal marriage, the eucharist in

[1] A religious colloquy at Worms between Catholics and Protestants in the interest of reunion.

[147]

both kinds, freedom from private mass and ceremonies, in order that we might be bound to recognize them as we did at Augsburg [in 1530], yet we shall not do it now, for then we did not exclude the pope, nor had we ourselves ordained priests; but that we do so is due to them, for they will not suffer our priests to be ordained by them except on conditions which they themselves are unable to grant. In fine, to make a treaty between us and the pope, is to make a treaty between God and Belial. Nothing will come of it."

"It is strange that no power in former ages was able to overthrow the papacy. Barbarossa and Frederick II were strong enough, but they couldn't do it. Today no imperial or royal power can hold up the tottering structure, for the pope's knavery has been revealed through the Word. Wherefore it is now plainly falling in ruins. For the papacy is essentially a lie, and a lie is the power of the devil for the destruction of every believer, just as the truth of God is the power of God for the salvation of every believer. I do not believe that the Turkish kingdom can be overcome by force, but some good man will appear, who will assail the dogma of Mohammed."

Luther's son brought to him a caterpillar in the garden. "What beautiful colors," said Luther, "this most noxious worm has! Thus also the pope is more beautifully arrayed than the emperor, but more harmful than the devil."

When some one remarked that the papists gladly read the books of Luther against the peasants and the Sacramentarians, the doctor replied: "They wouldn't be able to defend any of them, any more than they know how to defend any article of faith. They don't read their Bibles, but depend on Lombard's Sentences and what custom has introduced. But such authority is no longer accepted, for the proof is demanded. This they are unable to furnish; and indeed their whole system is founded on nothing but custom. For example, some one placed the consecrated water in the church, afterwards by imitation the practice came to prevail, and so it has remained."

"If the pope will throw away his crown and descend from his throne and primacy, and confess that he has erred, has destroyed the church and poured out innocent blood, then we will receive him into the church. Otherwise we must always regard him as Antichrist."

When Luther was so very ill at Scmalkal-
den[1] that all hope had been given up, and
he seemed at the point of death, he bade
farewell to the brethren, saying as his last
words: " This one thing preserve when I
am dead, namely, hatred towards the Roman
pontiff."

[1] In 1537.

24. MONKS AND MONASTICISM.

When the remark was made at table that the cowl was an Italian vest, Luther replied: " I should call it, rather, an Italian pest."

" Franciscans are our Lord God's lice, which the devil has put on his skin. Dominicans are fleas, which the devil has put in our Lord God's shirt."

" Christ often represents himself as our bridegroom and priest, a picture which is exceedingly full of comfort. Likewise he represents us as his bride and daughter, as in Hosea ii: ' And I will betroth thee unto me forever; yea, I will betroth thee unto me in righteousness, and in judgment and in loving kindness, and in mercies; I will even betroth thee unto me in faithfulness; and thou shall know the Lord.' Likewise in Ps. cx: ' The Lord hath sworn and will not repent, Thou art a priest forever after the order of Melchisedec.' Although he enters into spiritual marriage with us and swears that he will be our High Priest, nevertheless we do not believe it, but commit fornication with Baalim and choose for ourselves monkery. Fie on you, Moloch!"

"The opinion of those who think that the pope invented the doctrine of the celibacy of the priesthood for the purpose of enriching the priests, who would thus live without wives and children, is false; for it is by the outward semblance of holiness, which the celibate exhibits, that the pope has advanced himself and all his followers to the greatest opulence and has attained to such authority that he has kings under his feet."

"Monks are made by two causes: impatience and despair. For while they think that some of the evils among men can be borne, they despair of bearing with the utter depravity of the world. Therefore they flee the world and say: 'The world is too bad.'"

"God first created a single man, which was a good idea. Then he created woman, and therewith trouble began. And so the monks, acquiescing in God's first plan, live without wives, for they are wiser than God. If the emperor should root out this whole Franciscan order and keep their books as a perpetual memorial of their abominations, he would do a worthy deed. The Augustinians and Benedictines are nothing compared with them."

When Jonas complained of the nuns, that

they had thrown away their cowls and had
neglected the canonical hours, while they
made use of all the privileges of the convent,
Luther replied: " I am for the nuns. I
should like to comfort them with a letter.
Would that the nuns were all of that sort,
then their convents would become schools,
and they would be free to marry. For it is
hard for rulers and kings to give their daughters in marriage to husbands of lower rank,
and so they thrust them into convents.
It was an excellent law of Moses, whereby
only the first-born enjoyed royal authority,
while the others were subjects. So it is
even to-day in the East, and it would be a
most wholesome law for us."[1]

" The papists and Anabaptists teach that
if you would know Christ, you must be
alone, like a hermit, and not associate with
men. This is devilish advice against the
two great commandments. The first great
commandment requires faith and fear of
God, the second love to one's neighbor, which
means we ought to preach to and pray for
them and not flee into corners. Their
precept also opposes marriage, the household

[1] Saxony suffered greatly from the lack of this rule, which
was not introduced till the close of the 17th century, although
the Hohenzollern of Brandenburg were wise enough to adopt
it in 1473.

and the state, and is against the life of Christ
who was not willingly alone, but was always
in the midst of a throng of men, so that he
was never alone except when he prayed.
Goodbye to those who say:

' Keep to yourself apart,
Then you are pure in heart.' "

" The world does not know the hidden
treasures of God. It cannot be persuaded
that the maid working obediently and the
servant faithfully performing his duty, or
the woman rearing her children, are as good
as the praying monk who strikes his breast
and wrestles with the spirit."

" If the devil wishes to deprive one of his
reason, he secludes him, taking him away
from church, state and home, in all of which
places God is present protecting his own in
some particular occupation. A father once
decided that he would go to see his son, who
was a hermit. The devil, assuming the form
of a neighboring hermit, met the youth and
said to him: ' Tomorrow the devil will come
to you in the form of your father to persuade
you to desert this holy life.' Convinced of
this, the young man procured a hatchet,
and when his father approached, ran to him
and killed him. Wherefore I advise every

one to stick to his occupation and beware of solitude."

Luther's brother said that his uncle had caught two Franciscans in a wolftrap. Luther added: " In truth, they are the real wolves! "

25. THE DEVIL.

" Satan often said to me: ' What if your doctrine against the pope, the mass and the monks should be false? ' And he has often so pressed me that the sweat has broken out. At length I replied: ' Go and talk with God, who has ordered us to listen to this Christ. Christ must do all.' Therefore he who wishes to be a Christian must let Christ be responsible for everything."

" When Satan suggests that God is not gracious to me, it is blasphemy, because God has commanded me to expect remission of sins from this Christ; therefore he who does not do so makes God a liar. But I must say to the devil: ' Though I am a rogue, nevertheless Christ is good.' "

" Satan knows that we must die, nevertheless he is so furious against us that he tries constantly, to the best of his ability, to kill us, even as soon as we are born."

" The devil is as big as the world, as wide as the world; he reaches from heaven to hell."

" Early this morning," said Luther, " the devil was disputing with me about Zwingli, and I learned that it is not always well to be empty, that is, that one is better able to dispute with the devil on a full than on an empty stomach. For example, a certain bishop received a visit from his sister, who was tormented by anxious thoughts about her brother, who she feared was damned. After the bishop had tried without success to persuade her that her fears were groundless, he gave her plenty of good things to eat and drink for three days. At the end of this period he inquired how she felt. She replied that she was quite happy. 'Where are the fears that you had?'—'I have forgotten them.' Therefore eat, drink and enjoy yourselves! People tempted as this woman was should be well fed. Fornicators, however, ought to fast."

"I ought to be so happy that I should keep well from mere joy and be unable to get sick ; but Santa comes and disturbs me, if not in his own person, then in the person of Ki.[1] or some other. Heaven and earth, death and life, are great things, but faith in Christ is much greater."

"So we see the devil lies in wait for us on all sides, but we have Christ to help us. If we look to him there is no other God in heaven or on earth except the Saviour, but

[1] It is not certain to whom Luther referred.

if we lose sight of him there is no peace nor comfort. Wherefore all who are tempted should place Christ before their eyes as an example, for he must have been more tried than we are. I have often wondered how this could be when he knew that he was innocent, but the devil reproached him with keeping company with sinners. . . . Preaching is often a trial to me, for I think: ' Suppose you turn some creature the wrong way, then you are really guilty of his damnation.' Such a fear has often kept me in hell itself until God brought me back."

" Many demons are in the woods, the waters, in swamps and in deserts, in order to hurt men. Others, in the dense clouds, cause tempests, thunder and hail and infect the atmosphere. But philosophers and scientists ascribe these phenomena to nature and I know not what causes."

" I would rather be slain by the devil than by the emperor, for then I should die by a great lord. But he will get a piece of me that won't agree with him very well. He will spit it up again and then on the last day, I, in turn, will chew him up."

" Sancte Satan, ora pro nobis! Gracious Lord Devil, we have not sinned against you, nor did you make us nor give us life; wherefore, then, do you accuse[1] us so hard before God, as if you were holy and the supreme judge over God's true saints? Take your staff in your hand and go to Rome to your servant, whose god you are."

Commenting on the text, " Behold, I send you forth as sheep in the midst of wolves,"[2] Luther said: " Christ fights with the devil in a wonderful way; the devil has on his side extreme bravery, great numbers, prudence; Christ has weakness, a small number, contempt, simplicity, and yet Christ conquers. Thus he has willed that we should be sheep, and our adversaries wolves, but how unequal the contest, for one sheep to fight with ten or a hundred wolves! He sent twelve disciples into the world, twelve among so many wolves! That seems to me a wonderful war, an astounding battle, in which, moreover, the sheep are slain and the wolves survive. But along with their prey they will devour their death! Because God alone does marvellous things, and he will preserve his sheep in the midst of wolves and will destroy the jaws of the wolves forever."

Speaking of the Anabaptists, some one remarked: " It is remarkable that they are

[1] Job i and ii.   [2] Matt. x, 16.

so scornful of death and do not fear it."
But the doctor said: "Yes, they do not
know either sin or the wrath of God, they
are so blinded by the devil. Wherefore they
do not suffer, as do the saved, who know all
these things. For the devil keeps their ears
and minds occupied, so that no matter what
one says, they hear only what they have in
mind; thus also the devil infatuates the
foolish, so that they hear nothing except
what is in their own minds. When you say
to a fool: ' Drink! This is beer! ' he laughs:
' Ah,' he says, ' it is nothing! ' Thus Breitenbach, Pistoris and Agricola are clever enough
in the world's affairs, but here they are completely blinded and do not hear us, because
they have a preconceived opinion, and if we
pour anything into their ears, they laugh,
like natural fools. I discuss many things
concerning the law which condemns: Agricola cannot hear it; he has other principles
in his heart. When one says: ' Avarice
and usury are contrary to God,' Breitenbach
laughs and makes fun of us, as even the
Archbishop of Lund[1] said to Melanchthon,
that foreign nations ridiculed us for thinking
that fornication was a sin. And if the gospel

[1] John von Weeze, Archbishop of Lund, the envoy of
Charles V at the Congress of Frankfort, 1539, was a worldly
man.

[160]

had not come, all Germany would be full of that sort of thing, as already brothels were being publicly defended.[1] Whence it should be evident that Satan has great power, since he is able thus to blind and stultify men."

"The devil never ceases to disturb and worry men so that even at night and in their sleep he vexes them with disquieting dreams and anxieties to such a degree that the whole body is suffused with perspiration from mental anguish. Furthermore he even leads sleeping people from their beds to precipitous places, where, if angels did not guard them, they would fall and perish."

"Dreams arise thus: the human spirit cannot rest, for Satan is present when we sleep, though angels also are near. The devil can torment me so when I am asleep that the sweat breaks out.[2] I do not trouble myself about either dreams or signs. I have the Word, and that I let suffice. I would not wish to have an angel come to me; I would not believe him now, but the time might come in certain circumstances, when I might pray for such a thing. However I do not

---

[1] Augustine had written that harlots were necessary, and the Catholic Church had usually tolerated, and sometimes licensed them. See *The Open Court*, April, 1915, pp. 205ff.

[2] On this subject, *cf. American Journal of Psychology*, July 1913, pp. 363ff.

say that dreams and other signs are of any significance, nor do I worry about them, because we have already in Scripture what we are supposed to have. Sad dreams come from Satan, since everything which contributes to death and fear, murder and deceit, is the devil's handiwork. He has often driven me from prayer, and has poured into me such thoughts that I have run away. The best struggles that I have had with him, I have had in my bed by my Katie's side."

"The devil is a bad spirit, who rejoices when others suffer and is sad when they prosper. Men also are bad, but there are a few (choice tyrants and living devils) who feel no remorse for having done wrong nor any grief at the misfortunes of others." Then I[1] said: "But from whom has the devil learned such malice?" Luther did not reply to this, but remarked: "He will have to suffer, however, an eternal penalty." Then Schiefer: "There is with us a certain one who is offended by no article of the creed so much, as by that according to which God will punish eternally the devil and the wicked." Luther rejoined: "Yes, dear Doctor Schiefer, that is a great temptation,

[1] Mathesius, 1540.

[162]

concerning the eternal wrath of God! I thought about it earnestly at one time; God protect me, that my mind never again dwells on it, but upon Jesus Christ, in whom we see the mercy of the Father."

" I believe that the devil is in parrots, monkeys and apes, because they are able to imitate men so well."

On that day (August 20, 1538), Spalatin[1] related the tale of a witch's insolence, and how a girl at Altenburg shed tears of blood whenever the woman was present, for, even if she did not see her nor know of her, yet she felt her presence and shed tears. Luther answered: " One should hasten to put such witches to death. The jurists wish to have too many witnesses, despising these plain signs. Recently I had to deal with a matrimonial case, where the wife wished to poison her husband, so that he vomited lizards. When she was examined by torture she answered nothing, because such witches are dumb; they despise punishment and the devil does not let them speak. These facts show plainly enough that an example should be made of them to terrify others."

On August 25 (1538), they spoke much of

[1] George Spalatin, an old friend of Luther's, now pastor of a church at Altenburg in Electoral Saxony.

witches who stole eggs from hens and milk and butter. Luther said: " No mercy is to be shown them.[1] I myself would begin to burn them according to the law that the priests should begin to stone culprits. They say that they make the butter they steal rancid, and that those who eat it fall to the ground, and that the best way to vex such witches is to put the milk and butter on ice, for then they are reproved by Satan and forced to go to him. Village parsons and schoolmasters of old knew their arts and plagued them well. But Bugenhagen's way[2] is the best, to plague them with filth, stirring it often, so that all their things are soiled."

[1] Such sayings as these fanned the flames of the horrible persecution of witches by which hundreds of thousands of harmless persons lost their lives in the sixteenth century. Four witches were executed at Wittenberg in 1540.

[2] Bugenhagen, the Lutheran pastor of Wittenberg, defecated in the milk-pans. This antidote to witchcraft was recommended by St. Francis of Assisi to his follower Rufinus.

26. THE WORLD PREFERS SATAN TO THE GOSPEL.

" God is unable to rule the world, because the world is unwilling to be ruled by him, but prefers Satan, who understands how to manage people. But God has this advantage, that he knocks the world and Satan's kingdom in the world to pieces and grinds them to powder when they behave too badly."

" Merciful God, be gracious to me a sinner and grant me pardon and burial! For the world cannot bear with me nor I with the world."

" The more one preaches, the madder the world becomes, so that I wish that I might be compelled by some occasion to desist from preaching in order that Satan might have a freer opportunity, and one worthy of the world, to preach his own doctrines."

" The world wishes to deceive or to be deceived; therefore the world has no business with truth."

" The law is what we ought to do; the gospel however is of God, what God wishes to give. The first we are unable to accomplish, but the second we are able to receive, namely, through faith. But see what sort of beings men are! For the first, which they are unable to do, they want to do, while the second, which they ought to accept, they are unwilling to believe."

" The ingratitude of the world towards the gospel is indescribable and satanic. For the ministers are assailed, here by persecution, there by thanklessness, and unless we had a pious prince to defend us, our own people would torment us more than our open enemies. I could not succeed at present in getting a single city to maintain, by its own aid, a preacher. The whole city of Wittenberg gives in support of the precious gospel, for the entire year, four pfennigs[1] for each person. So it is everywhere. Cities which formerly feasted an unlimited number of monks, are unable now to support a single preacher. And yet papists support monks! But the scarcity of preachers will re-establish their authority. As they can now be had for nothing they are not respected; when carriages must be sent to bring them, and they take money for their preaching, then they will be highly regarded. I had not supposed that the devil could be so powerful in the world, had I not experienced it daily. Religion having been driven away, it is

[1] A pfennig is equal to about one-fourth of a cent.

superstition that has a hold on the people, not the gospel. The people of the world wish to be deceived by hobgoblins, since they pray again to the saints, burn candles and go upon pilgrimages; likewise they must have celibates, in other words, fornicators. For we have lost influence with them on account of our marrying. If I were younger I should give up preaching. I would rather take up some business and let others preach. But God will take vengeance upon this ingratitude, not by physical blows, but by condemning them on the last day to gehenna." After a moment Luther added: "Hold fast, Anthony,[1] and do not let these words frighten you. God will be your recompense and reward."

[1] Anthony Lauterbach.

27. GOD AND HIS GIFTS.

" Our Lord God must be a good man, to be fond of worthless fellows. I cannot like them, and yet I am one myself."

" A philosopher has said: ' God is a sphere, whose center is everywhere and whose circumference is nowhere.' Would that the fanatics and the nobles knew as much about God as this heathen! "

" As God creates all things from nothing, so he reduces all things to nothing. For what was Alexander the Great? Nothing, before he was born; what is he now? Nothing at all. God does the same thing through regeneration. Before he makes you a new man, that is, frees you from your impurity, into which you have come because of the weakness of your nature, it is necessary that you first become nothing; for God first makes you nothing through penitence, then something through faith."

" Would you like to know how God continues ruler of the world? By making the old lame and the young blind. Thus he remains master."

" Our God does not wish to be rich. He might be better off, if he wished, for if he should come to Ferdinand,[1] Duke George, or to the pope, and should say: 'Give me ten thousand florins or you will die this hour,' they would all reply: 'Yes, dear Lord, gladly, if only I may live!' Now since he does not do that sort of thing, they are not grateful to him for his gifts. If he bestowed his blessings more sparingly, we should be more grateful, as, for example, if he should take away from men their limbs, from this one a foot, from that one a hand, etc., and after some years should give them back to some, but not to others, the latter would, without doubt, soon give thanks to God and pray to him. But God's gifts are boundless. He heaps upon us all things at once in the greatest profusion. He gives us the liberal arts, and languages. The choicest books are to be had for a song. But woe to our sloth! For God will close his hand again and will bring it to pass that we who now neglect his true ministers will once more pay reverence to preachers of falsehood."

"God created the sparrows; therefore not one of them without his consent shall

---

[1] Ferdinand I was King of Bohemia and Hungary, and became emperor in 1556, on the abdication of his brother, Charles V. Duke George, of Albertine Saxony, remained hostile to Luther until his death in 1539. *Cf.* Smith, *Luther*, p. 221. Luther is speaking in 1532.

fall to the ground. God not only created men, but also gave his beloved son to suffer for them; consequently he will and must care far more for them than for the useless sparrows."

" As a father says to his family: ' Eat, drink and let me provide for you, so long as you are zealous to do my will,' so God does not care what you eat or drink or how you dress, but this he requires, namely, that you conform yourself to his will."

Observing his dog Tölpel,[1] Luther said: " Look at the dog! He hasn't a blemish on his whole body; he has fine bright eyes, strong legs, beautiful white teeth, a good stomach, etc. These are the highest bodily gifts, and God bestows them on such an unreasoning animal."

" It is a shameful thing and evidently an enchantment of the devil, that we trust more in human beings than in God. For example, I expect more good from my Katie, or from Professor Philip [Melanchthon], than from Christ. Why then should I fear him? But, you say, we are miserable sinners. To this Christ replies: ' Because I suffered, therefore you are baptized through me.' Consider also how very pleasantly he

[1] *I.e.*, Clown.

lived with his disciples, how patiently he bore with their idiosyncrasies. Furthermore it is written in Scripture: ' He who believes in him shall not be afraid.'[1] Fie on your unbelief, that we should flee from Christ, although he is gentler and kinder to us than any of our friends, brothers or parents! If therefore Christ seems to frighten any one, he should know that it is not Christ, but Satan."

" The best thing that theology can teach us is to know Christ. Therefore Peter says: ' Grow in the knowledge of Jesus Christ, for he is most merciful, most just and most wise.' "[2]

" Since our Lord God has made this transient kingdom, the sky, the earth and all things in them, so beautiful, how much more beautiful will he make the eternal kingdom."

Looking up at the sky one night Luther said: " He who has built such a vault without pillars must be a good master-workman."

" Even if Christ were only a man, yet would he be worthy of great honor, for he deserved well of us, doing much good and no evil, not to mention that he is very God and Saviour."

[1] Ps. lvi, 11.   [2] 2 Peter iii, 18.

One day when some birds were building a nest in his garden, but always flew away as we walked by, he said: "Dear little birds, don't fly away! I wish you well from my heart, if only you could trust me! Thus do we distrust God, who wishes us heartily well. He who has given his son for us will not slay us."

"The wicked cannot see the glory of God; indeed they cannot recognize his creations even when present. Thus when God simply overwhelms the wicked and all other men with the multitude and magnitude of his creatures, so that he may bring back by nature and by his beneficence those who are lost, they, on the contrary, only grow viler by reason of his benignity and care. What can God then do but let them go to hell? If any one brings us turkeys[1] or their eggs we exclaim and almost die with wonder. Just as he says: Consider the fowls of the air and the lilies of the field.[2] The male fish in the water casts forth his seed with a stroke of his tail, and the female, who is present, immediately conceives a hundred thousand fish. And all the philosophers cannot give

[1] Interesting as one of the first allusions in European literature to the turkey, recently imported from America. Luther spoke in the autumn of 1533.

[2] Matthew vi, 26ff.

a reason for this, but only Moses, when he wrote: ' God spoke and it was done;[1] Increase and multiply,[2] and it was thus.' "

" Our Lord God and the devil have two different methods of procedure. Our Lord God first terrifies, then restores and consoles, to the end that the flesh may die, and the spirit live. Thus also the good angels frighten people and afterwards console them. On the other hand the devil caresses men in their sins, and afterwards brings them to despair; he exhilarates the flesh and saddens the spirit; for at the time the wrong is done there is no remorse, but afterwards there remains a sad and despairing conscience."

" How wonderful it is that God is so rich! He gives enough, but we don't appreciate it. He gave to Adam the whole world, but that was nothing; what he cared about was a single tree, and so he must ask why God had forbidden it to him. It is the same to-day. God has given us enough to learn in his revealed Word, but we leave that and seek after his hidden will, which however, we are unable to learn. Therefore it is no more than right if in acting thus we are utterly ruined."

" Three very useful instruments of singu-

[1] Genesis, i, 3ff.   [2] Genesis, i, 22ff.

lar benefit have been given to man: the magnet, the clock and fire. I cannot admire and extol sufficiently the steel and stone as generators of fire, and I wish that some one would publicly commend the magnet, which loves iron as a husband his spouse."

28. THE BIBLE.

" There are two things in the world which Christians ought to attend to: the word of God and the work of God."

" That the Bible is the word of God and not of man, that it is God's book and not man's, is proved by the fact that all things in the world, what they are and how they are conditioned, are described in the book of Genesis by Moses, and everything remains exactly as God created it. Moreover, Julius Cæsar, Augustus, Alexander, the kingdoms of the Egyptians, Babylonians, Persians, Greeks and Romans have passed away, and though they all wished to blot out and destroy this book, and eagerly sought to do so, yet they did not succeed; the book remained unharmed in spite of them all. Who sustains it, or who could have preserved it against so great might and power? Homer and Vergil are old books, but not as compared with the Bible. Likewise baptism, the sacrament of the Lord's supper, and the ministry, that is, the whole worship enjoined by the First Commandment, have remained in spite of so many tyrants and heretics. Our Lord God has sustained them with peculiar and wonderful power, because preaching, baptism and the communion are so necessary that no one is able to oppose them."

"The litany of litanies is the Lord's prayer. The learning of the learned is the decalogue. The virtue of the virtuous is the creed. For as the Lord's prayer excellently and beautifully asks and demands, thus the decalogue excellently, fully and beautifully teaches and exhorts, and the creed fully, excellently and beautifully operates and exercises all. Thus these three make a man perfect and absolute in thought, word and deed; that is, they nourish and bring to the highest perfection his mind, tongue and body."

"The New Testament throws light upon the Old as the day lights up the night. Since the Jews neither believe nor accept it, it is impossible for them to understand the prophecies, except as histories."

"Money is the devil's Word, by which he creates everything in the world, as God creates all things by the true Word."

"Judith seems to me to be a tragedy, wherein is described the end of tyrants, while Tobias seems like a comedy, which speaks much of women; the former illustrates the conduct of state affairs, the latter is an example of household management."

" One must hold fast to the Word, so that if I should behold all the angels and hear them telling me not to believe some verse of Scripture, not only ought I not to be moved by them, but I ought to close my eyes and ears, for they would be unworthy of being looked upon or listened to."

" I would give the world to have the stories of the antediluvian patriarchs also, that we might see how they lived, preached and suffered. . . . I have taught and suffered too, but only fifteen, twenty or thirty years; they lived seven or eight hundred years and how they must have suffered! "

" The ingratitude and vanity of the world are inexpressible. Before the New Testament[1] was translated, everyone was eager to have it done so that he could read it, and when it was done it was only four weeks before all were clamoring for a translation of the Old Testament. That[2] lasted four weeks when the cry arose for the Psaltery,[3] which lasted another four weeks. The trans-

[1] Luther's translation of the New Testament appeared in 1522.
[2] Luther means the Pentateuch, which appeared in 1523.
[3] This appeared in 1524.

lation of Ecclesiasticus,[1] which is giving me much trouble, will do for another four weeks, and then the people will keep on demanding something new, until they fall into some error."

" He who will become a theologian now has a great advantage in having the German Bible. That is so clear that he can read it without any hindrance. Then let him read Melanchthon's *Commonplaces* industriously and thoroughly until he has mastered it. When he has read these two books he will be a theologian whom neither the devil nor any heretic can shake, and all divinity lies open to him to read what he likes with edification. If he cares to he can read my commentaries on Romans, Galatians and Deuteronomy, which will give him eloquence and a copious vocabulary. But you will find no book under the sun in which the whole of theology is so well summed up as in the *Commonplaces*. Read all the fathers and commentators on the Canon Law — they are nothing! There is no better book than this of Melanchthon's except Scripture. He is more concise than I; he argues and instructs; I am garrulous and rhetorical. If people follow my advice

[1] Luther was working at Ecclesiasticus at the time of this saying, 1532.

they will only print my doctrinal books, though indeed they may read the others for history to see how things went, for at first it was not so easy as it now is."

"I should prefer all my books to perish that only the Bible might be read, for other books take up our attention and make us neglect the Bible. Even Brenz made such a commentary on twelve chapters of Luke that it irks the reader to look at the text. Such also is my commentary on Galatians. I am surprised that any one should try to improve on those eloquent writings. Who would buy such volumes? Even if he bought them who would read them? Even if he read them who would profit by them?"

"How does it happen that we do not believe the Word of God, in spite of the fact that everything has happened as is written in the Scriptures, even to the article on the resurrection of the dead? It is because of original sin."

"The sacred Scripture does not deal with gross sinners, such as publicans and harlots, for their sins even the heathen can judge, but with those spiritual immoralities which before the world have the name of respectability and honesty."

"John in his gospel represents Christ as

being God, reasoning *a priori*, from the cause to the effect; Paul reaches the same conclusion *a posteriori*, from the effect to the cause. John says: 'In the beginning was the Word,'[1] also, 'It is my father that honoreth me; of whom ye say that he is your God.'[2] Paul, however, says: 'They tempted Christ in the desert; therefore Christ is God;'[3] and in Acts xx: 'Take heed therefore unto yourselves, etc.' "[4]

" The life of Christ should be considered from three points of view: first as history, second as a gift, third as an example and inspiration. History presents the most powerful examples of faith and infidelity."

" Christ seems to have been called Nazarene[5] from the Hebrew word[6] meaning elect, set apart, sanctified, consecrated with a new crown."

" The reader of the Scriptures should be a humble person, who shows reverence and fear towards the Word of God, who constantly says: 'Teach me, teach me, teach me.' The Spirit resists the proud; even though they are zealous and preach Christ for a time without fault, nevertheless, if they are proud,

---

[1] John i, 1.
[2] John viii, 54.
[3] Hebrews iii, 1-11.
[4] Acts xx, 28.
[5] Matthew ii, 23.
[6] Numbers vi.

God excludes them from the Church. Wherefore every proud person is a heretic, if not *de facto*, nevertheless, potentially. It is, however, difficult for him who is richly endowed with talents not to be arrogant. But those whom God has adorned with great gifts he leads into most severe temptations, that they may see how helpless they are. Paul bore a thorn in the flesh,[1] lest he become proud, and unless Philip[2] were thus afflicted he would have wonderful opinions. If James[3] and Agricola[4] should become proud and despise their teachers I fear that there would be no getting on with them. I know the insolence of Münzer, Zwingli and Carlstadt. Pride drove the angel from heaven, and it spoils many a preacher. Therefore it is humility that we need in the study of sacred literature."

"The Hebrew tongue is altogether despised because of impiety or, perhaps, because people despair of learning it. . . . Without this language there can be no understanding of Scripture, for the New Testament, although written in Greek, is full of

[1] 2 Cor. xii, 7.

[2] Melanchthon, a sickly person.

[3] Schenk, accused of antinomianism.

[4] John Agricola, 1494–1566, an antinomian. Smith, *Luther*, 282ff.

Hebraisms. It is rightly said that the Hebrews drink from the fountains, the Greeks from the streams and the Latins from the pools. I am no Hebrew grammarian, nor do I wish to be, for I cannot bear to be hampered by rules; but I am quite at ease in the language, for whoever has the gift of tongues, even though he cannot forthwith turn anything into another language, or interpret it, yet has a wonderful gift of God. The translators of the Septuagint were unskilled in Hebrew, and their version is therefore extremely poor, even though literal. We prefer to it the version of Jerome, even though we confess that he who reviled Jerome as a good Jew, was mistaken and did him wrong. But he has this excuse that after the Babylonian captivity the language was so corrupted that it could not be restored."

When he was correcting his version of II Maccabees he said: " I am so hostile to this book and to Esther that I wish they did not exist; they have too much Jewish and heathen nonsense."

" Genesis is a charming book and has wonderful stories! I cannot understand it all, however. I shall need to have been dead several years before I shall thoroughly understand the meaning of creation and the

omnipotence of God. For we cannot grasp
it and must be content to leave it, like that
judge who prayed: 'I believe on God Almighty.' He thought that that was God's
name; like the nun who called Christ
'Master Scimus' and 'Master Clic.'[1] For
no one can study out the meaning of that
word creation, though even the heathen have
this thought: There must be a first cause,
which makes and governs all things."

Asked whether it was the same woman who
anointed the Lord in the house of Lazarus
and in that of Simon, Luther replied: "Oh,
it is certain that it was the same one; it
is immaterial that in one place it is written
that Judas murmured,[2] while in another[3]
this is omitted. There is also this difference:
he complained from malice, the others from
simplicity. But here is a knotty point that
I would like to have cleared up, whether the
woman mentioned in Luke vii,[4] from whom
Christ drove the devils is the same as the
one who is called a sinner.[5] She was, however, not a prostitute, for the Jews did not

---

[1] There are two prayers in the Catholic ritual, one of which
begins "Magister Scimus" (Lord, we know), the other
"Magister dic" (Master, speak). The nun misread the
latter "Magister clic."

[2] John xii, 5.

[3] Matt. xxvi, 6.

[4] Luke viii, 2.

[5] Luke vii, 37, 39.

have prostitutes; but she is called a sinner because she had been possessed of devils, since the Jews called all obsessed persons sinners; though any one who was under a penalty was also called a sinner. Perhaps it was some light-hearted wench, a bit indiscreet in her talk." — " Verily, I say unto you, wheresoever this gospel shall be preached mention shall be made of that woman."[1] When asked why Christ added this, he replied: " That it might be seen that he greatly valued works of mercy, especially when done to help a human being who lies on the death bed. In the second place it is an allegory. For Judas overthrows all that is good and promotes all that is bad. That is the way of the devil and the world; they praise what ought to be condemned and condemn what ought to be praised. Thus the devil is merciful where he ought to harden his heart; he is hard where he ought to be merciful. The world punishes where it ought not to punish, and is lax where it ought to be strict."

Luther said: " Paul does not use such big words as Demosthenes, but he speaks properly and uses significant words. He did right in not being very involved or preten-

[1] Matt. xxvi, 13; Mark xiv, 9.

tious, else every one would want to talk that way."

Luther asked Jonas about a passage in Genesis,[1] and how it was credible that when Sarah was ninety years old she should have been taken by King Abimelech. Jonas answered that ninety years at that time was as twenty with us. " No," answered the doctor, " for Abraham was nearer the time of David than the time of Adam, and in David's time the years of a man's life were said to be seventy or eighty. The spring of the world was before the flood. After that its flower faded. In short, the Scripture is an inscrutable book. One can never fathom it."

" ' They pierced my hands and my feet.'[2] The Jews simply laugh at this text about the crucifixion of Christ; indeed, they say that he was not crucified, because neither Moses nor the prophets indicate that this method

[1] Genesis xx, 2 and xviii, 11f.

[2] Psalm xxii, 17, Greek, Latin and English revised versions. This remarkable verse, occurring in a Psalm which strongly colored the Gospel narratives of the passion, has been quoted as a prophecy of the crucifixion by Irenaeus, Justin Martyr, Augustine, Calvin, Bossuet and a host of others. R. Kittel (*Die Psalmen*, 1914, pp. 84ff, 92) shows that the verse really does refer to crucifixion, which was practiced by the Persians, from whom it was borrowed by the Carthaginians and Romans. Psalm xxii, is supposed to have originated in the period of Jewish subjection to the Persians.

of execution was used by the Jews, but only stoning and burning. I answer them that the Romans put to death not according to the laws of the Jews, but according to those of the Gentiles. For to-day in Syria men are hung, as in Hungary they are impaled. Therefore the argument of the Jews that Christ was not crucified, because they do not read in Moses of this species of torment, is invalid. Moses does, indeed, speak of hanging on a tree,[1] but not of piercing the hands and feet."

[1] Deuteronomy xxi, 23.

29. PREACHERS AND PREACHING.

" He who has but a single word of Scripture and is unable to make from it an entire sermon, ought never to be a preacher."

" Sermons should be adapted to the occasion and to the audience. For example, a certain preacher declared that it was wicked for a wife to obtain a wet-nurse for her child, and devoted his whole sermon to this, though he had in his parish only a lot of poor spinsters, to whom the admonition did not apply. A similar case was that of the preacher who, in an old ladies' home among old wives, spoke in praise of matrimony and admonished his hearers to get married."

" A preacher should be skilled in both logic and oratory, that is, it is necessary for him both to teach and to exhort. And when he is about to treat a subject, he should first set it forth, then define it; third, adduce passages of Scripture in support of it; fourth, illustrate it with examples from the Bible or elsewhere, fifth, adorn it with parables; sixth, administer reproof to the wicked, the disobedient, the slothful, and others."

" I know no better tonic for me than anger. If I wish to write, pray, or preach well, then

I need to become angry; thus all my being is refreshed, my wits are sharpened, and all temptations flee."

" To preach Christ is a hard task and one fraught with the greatest danger. If I had known this in time I should never have become a preacher, but should have said with Moses: ' Send whom thou wilt send.'[1] No one could have induced me to undertake it. Therefore the Bishop of Brandenburg said to me with truth: ' Doctor, I have told you that you should keep still; you will get into trouble, for it is a matter that touches the Holy Christian Church.'[2] I have indeed gotten into trouble, for I who once enjoyed the greatest freedom from care, have kindled against myself hatred throughout the world."

" To me a long sermon is an abomination, for the desire of the audience to listen is destroyed, and the preacher only defeats himself. On this account I took Dr. Bugenhagen severely to task, for although he preaches long sermons with spontaneity and pleasure, nevertheless it is a mistake."

When Katie said she could understand her minister Polner's preaching better than Bugenhagen's because the latter wandered

[1] Ex. iv, 13.
[2] In 1518. See Smith, *Luther's Correspondence*, i, pp. 73f, 87f.

too far from his text, Luther remarked: "Bugenhagen preaches as you women usually talk; he says whatever occurs to him. Jonas used to say, ' Don't hail every soldier you meet.' That is right. Bugenhagen often takes along everyone whom he meets with him. He is foolish to try to say all that occurs to him. Let him take care to keep to the text and attend to what is before him and make people understand that. Those preachers who say whatever comes into their mouths remind me of a maid going to market. When she meets another maid she stops and chats a while, then she meets another and talks with her, too, and then a third and a fourth, and so gets to market very slowly. So with preachers who wander off the text; they would like to say everything at one time, but they can't."

"A preacher should have the following qualifications: 1. Ability to teach. 2. A good mind. 3. Eloquence. 4. A good voice. 5. A good memory. 6. Power to leave off. 7. Diligence. 8. Wholesouled devotion to his calling. 9. Willingness to be bothered by everyone. 10. Patience to bear all things. In ministers nothing is seen more easily or more quickly than their faults. A preacher may have a hundred virtues, yet they may all be obscured by a single defect, the world is now so bad. Dr. Jonas has all the attributes of a good preacher, but people cannot forgive the good man for hawking and spitting so often."

" As the world would have him, six things are necessary to a preacher: 1. He must have a fine pronunciation. 2. He must be learned. 3. He must be eloquent. 4. He must be a handsome person, whom the girls and the young ladies will like. 5. He must take no money, but have money to give. 6. He must tell people what they like to hear."[1]

When mention was made of the opposition which ministers of the Word suffer from some of those learned in the law, he said: " Preachers ought to suffer and must do so. That has been the case since the beginning of the world, for they have reviled even thee "— pointing with his finger to a picture of Christ hanging near the table — "and yet thou remainest forever the greatest preacher, while they are utterly destroyed; thus we preachers also survive, while they are all ruined. They are kings of this world only, but thou, Lord Christ, art king and priest forever. It is a dreadful thing, that people should have so great a dislike for

[1] This was said in 1542, while the preceding saying belongs to the year 1532.

that which they cannot get along without; for they must have some one to preach the Word, through which God exerts his power and accomplishes his ends: He does nothing except through the Word as preached in the church. The devil hates not only the pious priests, but also the bad ones, for he is afraid that they may become devout and do him harm. Yet he is not so much afraid of the priests as he is of the Word and the sacraments, for it is these that do him harm. But of course there would be no sacraments, if there were no priests. But since there are priests still, he must be on his guard against them. It is for this reason that he hates the preachers so and pursues them, wherever he can."

"When you are going to preach, first pray and say: 'Dear Lord, I would preach for thy honor; though I can do nothing good of myself, do thou make it good.' Don't think about Melanchthon or Bugenhagen or me or any learned man, and don't try to be learned in the pulpit. I have never been troubled because I could not preach well, but I am overawed to think that I have to preach before God's face and speak of his infinite majesty and divine being. Therefore be strong and pray."

" A preacher can get no more effective text than the first commandment: ' I am the Lord thy God.' With it he can preach hell-fire to the froward and heavenly peace to the pious, punish the bad and comfort the good alike. My friend Forster says that he is moved by only three preachers, by me, by Cordatus and by Rörer, and that our gifts are supplementary, so that where one fails the other succeeds, just as different knives are adapted to different purposes."

" It used to be thought womanish or childish to mention Christ in the pulpit. Scotus, Bonaventura, Occam, Aristotle and Plato reigned there."

" Who know their subject can speak easily, for art follows comprehension of the subject. I can never compose a sermon by the rules of rhetoric."

Turning to George Major Luther warned him against timidity, and not to preach to those who were wiser than himself but to instruct the common people. " A preacher should bare his breast and give the simple folk milk, for every day a new need of first principles arises. One should be diligent with the catechism and serve out only milk, leaving the strong wine of high thoughts for private discussion with the wise. In my sermons I do not think of Bugenhagen, Jonas and Melanchthon, for they know as much as I do, so I preach not to them but to my little Lena and Hans and Elsa. It would be a foolish gardener who would attend to one flower to the neglect of the great majority."

When Erasmus Alber was about to take his departure for the Mark,[1] he asked Doctor Martin how he should preach in the presence of the prince. Luther replied: "Let all your sermons be very plain and simple. Think not of the prince, but of the uncultivated and ignorant people. The prince himself is made of the same stuff as they! If in my preaching I should address myself to Philip I should do no good. I preach very simply to the uneducated and it suits everybody. Though I know Greek, Hebrew and Latin, these languages I keep for use among ourselves, and then we get them so twisted that our Lord God is amazed."

"Every priest must have his private sacrifices. Therefore Bugenhagen[2] sacrifices his auditors with his long sermons, for we are his victims. He did it finely today."[3]

---

[1] In 1537. He had been appointed court preacher to the Margrave of Brandenburg.

[2] The parish priest at Wittenberg. [3] January 26, 1533.

[193]

" Love of glory does the mischief. Zwingli was so very eager for glory that he wrote that he had learned nothing from me. I have no desire to show that he got any part of his teaching from me, for it has not prospered. Thus Œcolampadius thought himself so wise that he could learn nothing from me — he even thought he excelled me. Likewise Carlstadt says: 'It is nothing to me what you think.' And Münzer preached against two popes, a new one and an old one, and he compared me to Saul, saying that I began well, but adding that the spirit of God had departed from me. I pitied Œcolampadius, and yet I wondered how it was possible for a man of good heart to vomit forth against me such bitter things. Therefore let all preachers beware of seeking glory in sacred literature, for otherwise they are lost. Leave glory to Vergil and Cicero! Scripture desires humility and a contrite heart, therein dwells the Holy Spirit."

" He who wishes to rule the world by the Gospel should become a fool. God must put blinders on preachers, as we do on horses, when he wishes to send them against Satan and the world. For what equality is there between Satan and man? Compare Peter and Rome: Peter a fisherman of Bethsaida,

Rome the meeting-place of the wisest men; and this dear Peter was to reform! Who wouldn't laugh at that?"

"It is best not to preach long sermons, and to speak simply and like a child, for one must preach only to little Hans and little Martin and the young. To undertake to preach to the doctor[1] and Philip is wrong, although I understand very well that they think, since I am there, they must also be learned. Ah no! Preaching is meant for the children! In the school one may be learned."

"Christ had an extremely simple way of talking, and still he was eloquence itself. The prophets, to be sure, are not very rhetorical, but they are much more difficult. Therefore simple speech is the best and truest eloquence."

"When Mörlin,[2] Medler[3] or Jacob[4] preaches, it is just as when the plug is drawn from a full cask; the liquid runs out as long as there is any left within. But such volubility of tongue doesn't really lay hold of the audience, though it delights some, nor is it even in-

[1] *I. e.* Luther.
[2] Joachim Mörlin, deacon at Wittenberg.
[3] Nicholas Medler, at this time Superintendent at Naumburg.
[4] Text: Magister Jacob. Who he was is not clear.

[195]

structive. It is better to speak distinctly, so that what is said may be comprehended."

"A bee is a small animal which makes sweet honey, but which nevertheless can sting. So a preacher has the sweetest consolations, yet when aroused to anger he can say biting and stinging things."

30. WYCLIF AND HUSS.

"Wyclif and Huss fought merely against the pope's manner of life, therefore they did not succeed, since they themselves were sinners like the papists. But I attacked his doctrine; thereby have I beaten him, since the most important thing is not how we live, but what we believe and teach."

"The blood of Huss condemns the papist today. For he was a learned man, as appears from his pamphlet on the church,[1] and I love him. He died not like the Anabaptists but like Christ. Even if human weakness could be seen in him, yet the power of God overcame it. The battle between the spirit and the flesh in Christ and in Huss is sweet to see. All testimony says that Huss was most learned and Jerome of Prague most eloquent; more cannot be said. Huss knew more than the whole world and was condemned, though innocent. From that time the papal power began to fall and retrograde." Schiefer added: "The city of Constance is wretched." Luther: "I believe God has punished it for having condemned Huss."

[1] See: John Huss: *The Church, translated by D. S. Schaff.* New York, 1915.

" It is our Lord's way to proceed in accordance with the text: ' My strength is made perfect in weakness.'[1] Thus he first makes the earth a rough mass, and afterwards forms all things one by one. He does not create man immediately, but first makes the land. Likewise he first hides the seed in the earth, from which the tree grows but slowly. He could make everything at once by a single word, but he does not wish to. It is not his way, to make something out of nothing. Thus our reform movement was weak at first, but it grew from day to day. John Huss was the seed; he must first die, burned at the stake. Would not that seem to the human reason great weakness? But see what, after a hundred years, has come of it! "

When Agricola read some letters of John Huss, which he had translated, letters which breathed the noblest spirit, patience and eloquence and which described how he had been tortured in prison by an attack of the stone and was spurned by King Sigismund, Luther expressed his admiration for the spirit of Huss, who had written such things with so great fortitude: " He was a rare man. His death has been well avenged, for soon

[1] 2 Cor. xii, 9.

afterwards Sigismund suffered the greatest misfortunes: His wife became a harlot for the whole court, and the Bohemians devastated Germany everywhere; they set Nuremberg on fire, and penetrated even as far as Zeitz. The Germans several times showed their heels."

31. PHILIP MELANCHTHON.

" In the Acts of the Apostles you see our pictures. In James we see a Melanchthon who was so conservative that he wished to keep the law; in Peter I am portrayed, as one who burst through it with, ' Why would ye burden them with the law? ' Melanchthon acts in charity and faith and lets himself be smitten. I smite and spare no one. So God operates in diversity of gifts. Melanchthon is too moderate, he only encourages the papists. He wishes to serve all men by love. If the papists used me as they do him I would hit back."

" The most excellent of the prophets are Isaiah and Daniel. I am Isaiah, Philip[1] is Jeremiah. Jeremiah was always worrying for fear he scolded too much, and so is Philip."

" Melanchthon is lighter than I and therefore more easily moved if things don't go his way. I am heavier and stupider and am not so much affected by things I cannot remedy. Time heals many things, but worrying about them does not. In treating Scripture I am more vehement than Melanch-

[1] Luther usually speaks of Melanchthon by his first name.

[200]

thon though he is quite bitter in his pamphlet on the church. I mean to say the substance of his book is strong, but the words do not seem to me to correspond to the sense, perhaps because I do not understand the force of Latin. I rough hew and Melanchthon planes."

Luther said to Melanchthon: " Do you wish to obey God or man? " " God," he replied, " for it is better to fall into the hands of the Lord than into the hands of men." Luther continued: " Will you hear God's Word immediately or through a man? " — " Through a man."—" Then I command you in God's name to stop studying and working until I bid you do otherwise, for God wills that we keep a sabbatical rest."

While we were singing, the doctor remarked: " Every one is rushing into print. So many books! "—" Aye " assented several, " dialectic books." — " Fool books," continued Luther, " Melanchthon alone writes dialectic; all drink from this source but no one follows Melanchthon, much less overtakes him."

Speaking of Melanchthon it was said that he used great moderation in the Evangelical cause. Luther said: " The little man is pious, and when he does wrong it is not with malice prepense. In his way he has accomplished much but he has been unfortunate in the dedications of his books.[1] To judge by results I should say that my way was the better, to speak and hit out like a boy. Blunt wedges rive hard knots."[2]

"Melanchthon kept me a day at Schmalkalden[3] with his godless and shabby astrology, because it was a new moon. Once he would not cross the Elbe during a new moon. But we are lords of our stars."

"Vergil has made many bad poets, Melanchthon many bad logicians and I many bad theologians. Some write by a wooden rule and think if they have three propositions they have a syllogism."

"I think that Philip takes up the study of astrology just as I take a strong drink of beer, whenever I have heavy thoughts."

"Little, trivial matters bother me very much; large affairs, however, do not, for I say to myself: 'This is beyond you, you cannot grasp it, so let it go.' That is not the way with Philip however. He is not

[1] Melanchthon had dedicated books to Albert of Mainz, and to Henry VIII.

[2] *Malo nodo malus cuneus*, a proverb several times used by Luther. This rendering is borrowed from Shakespeare, *Troilus and Cressida*.

[3] February, 1537. *Cf.* Smith, *Luther*, p. 308ff.

moved by things that trouble me, but rather by weighty affairs of politics and religion. Only private matters rest heavily on me. Thus do gifts vary."

"Philip has done more in logic than any one in a thousand years. I knew the subject theoretically, but Philip has taught me to apply it concretely. No one can pay Philip for his work. He has to live in a poor house.[1] Perhaps it is adequate for advancing the gospel. He is diffident. God help him. He will get to heaven, and thus he will be paid; the world will not pay him for his pains and his labor."

"Philip also has completely lost the good will of the papists. For a while he was determined to handle the matter with his gentle reasonableness; now he sees that that will not avail with knaves."

When the conversation fell upon the liberality of Melanchthon, Schiefer said: "Doctor, if Philip were bishop of Salzburg, would he remain so generous?" "Most certainly," replied Luther, "for he has the true knowledge of Christ Jesus."

Luther's wife said: "Philip has received more in gifts from the king of England,

[1] Luther is speaking in 1532. Melanchthon's new house, which is still standing, was completed in 1537. Tischreden, Weimar Ed., ii, 128.

namely, 500 gulden, — while we received only 50, — and from the elector 100, besides 80 thalers from I know not whom." The doctor replied: "And he expends much upon his friends and upon strangers. He distributes this treasure. And he would be worthy of it, if he should be given a kingdom, so great a man is he and so deserving of reward from the Roman empire and the church, not only throughout Germany but also in other lands."

"Philip has written good books, and no one will write better on penance. And the commentaries on Romans and Colossians, and the Commonplaces, those are divine books, and the [Augsburg] Confession and the Apology! Ah, how fine it is to study now, as compared with former times!"

Schiefer said of Melanchthon: "He is a great man and willing to take upon himself a large amount of work. Wherefore the youths ought to spare him, and not burden him so much with their writings. But our youth are little wiser than swine." To this Luther added: "Philip does not observe the sabbath, but is a common drudge and the servant of servants."

32. HERETICS.

" Upon brothers who withdraw themselves from us,[1] we are unable to inflict more severe punishment than to let them go their way and do what they will. One exception, however, we make to this: we shall not consent to be of their company and to call them brothers. And so we send them to hell in their own finery."

On April 5, 1532, at dinner, Luther said concerning heretics: " I like violent fanatics; they destroy themselves. Paul is the wisest man since Christ; he says: ' A man that is a heretic, after the first and second admonition, reject.' "[2]

" False brethren we shall in no wise endure, while life remains to us; but if they are willing to confess their wickedness and admit that they are without Christ, then we will endure all things from them, even though they kill us."

" By far the greatest battle that Christians have to fight is that with the false brethren, and the fight is so hard because, although they are not Christians, they wish to be known as such. If they were willing

[1] *I.e.* schismatics.   [2] Tit. iii, 10.

to call themselves Pilates, Judases and Herods, that is, if they were willing to lay aside the name Christian, we would endure all the injuries they dared to bring upon us; war would cease and there would be peace between them and us. Since, however, they insist on being regarded as Christians, we must fight them and in no wise suffer them to speak and do with impunity what is not befitting Christians. For we claim for ourselves through the Word the dominion over consciences, and we will not permit it to be taken from us."

" I believe that the Anabaptists, who talk so volubly about their being angels of God sent to purge the world in the year 1540, are incendiaries, for they kill[1] themselves and confess nothing, and they believe themselves to be martyrs like the Donatists,[2] who threw themselves into the water from towers and rocks and begged passers-by to kill them and make them martyrs. Against them Augustine disputed, saying: ' It is not the punishment, but the cause, that makes a martyr.' "

" Agricola still calls himself the son of God. That is the peculiarity of all heretics, to believe that they have the spirit of God,

[1] *I.e.*, by refusing to recant and submitting to death for heresy.
[2] Heretics who were obnoxious to St. Augustine.

and to know nothing of original sin. They think themselves saints. In myself, however, I find no sanctity, but rather great weakness. Hardly have I begun to be tempted when I recognize the spirit, but the flesh fighteth against it. Idolatry is an offense against the first commandment! I should like very much to feel myself formally justified, but I cannot find it in me." Bugenhagen added " Doctor, I don't find it in myself either."

33. CONCERNING LIES

" Lies are of four kinds: First the sportive lie, a hearty, ludicrous jest, which affords amusement or cheers up those who are depressed. Second the charitable lie, a good useful lie, which springs from the desire to help our kindred or our friends, as for example, that of Abraham, when he said that his wife Sarah was his sister,[1] or of Michal, when she saved David,[2] or of Elisha, when he said to the Syrians: ' This is not the way, nor is this the city.'[3] The third kind is the noxious lie, which seeks to deceive and injure, according to the way of the world. The fourth is the irreverent lie, by which God is blasphemed. The first two are praiseworthy, since they do no harm; the last two are intolerable, since they offend both man and God. There is also another kind, namely, the necessary lie, although it does not differ much from the second kind, the charitable; and this may be resorted to without fault, if it is not accompanied by an oath such as ' really,' ' truly,' ' by God,' or the like."

[1] Gen. xx, 2.   [2] 1 Sam., xix, 13.   [3] 2 Kings, vi, 19.

"A liar is far worse than a murderer and does more harm, because he deceives, while the murderer is unable to deceive. Judas, however, was both a liar and a murderer, like his father the devil."

"It is a marvel that when Judas was eating at table with Christ and the disciples he should not have blushed with shame, when Christ said:[1] 'One of you shall betray me.' The other disciples had not the slightest suspicion that Judas was about to betray Christ; each one feared indeed that he himself would be the traitor rather than Judas, to whom Christ had entrusted the purse and the whole business management, on account of which he was held in the highest esteem among the apostles."

[1] Mat., xxvi, 21.

34. TEMPTATIONS.

" Temptation therefore saves us from pride, and at the same time increases our knowledge of Christ and his gifts, for with it God has given me a glorious victory. By it I conquered my monkery and monastic vows and the mass and all such abominations. How could God do otherwise? Since neither the pope nor the emperor can quell me the devil must do it, or my virtue will perish for lack of an enemy. Peter finely says, ' Ye know that the same afflictions are accomplished in your brethren that are in the world,'[1] for we are not alone but there are many who have the same trials. We are not without consolation; our victory remains through remission of sins. We who know our sins have no cause to fear, but only those who don't know them. It all depends on ' rightly dividing the word of truth,'[2] as St. Paul says, for we should not be terrified by the hard sayings and examples, but should take to ourselves the promises.

" Therefore, dear Schlaginhaufen, suffer temptation for God's glory and pray no more for freedom except as it may please

[1] 1 Peter, v. 9.　　　　[2] 2 Tim., ii, 15.

him. It is profitable that we should know the arts of the devil. He takes the smallest sins and exaggerates them. Once he tortured and almost throttled me with what Paul wrote Timothy,[1] so that my heart almost melted in my body. 'You were the cause,' said he, 'of many monks and nuns leaving the cloister.' He completely took the thought of justification out of my mind, and held up one text after another against me, both from the law and the gospel. Bugenhagen was with me, and I put the text to him. He began to doubt himself, though he knew not how hard I was pressed and how I feared and consumed the night with heavy heart. The next day he came to me and said: 'I am right angry, for I have examined the text carefully and the argument is ridiculous.' So it is when one is himself, but not otherwise."

"The temptations that come during life, which great saints like Paul suffer, are far more severe than the pains of death."

[1] About young widows waxing wanton and marrying? 1 Tim. v, 11.

35. QUESTIONS.

These are only a few of the multitude of questions that were put to Luther by his companions and friends. His answers to such questions make up a large part of his table talk.

When asked whether a priest might refuse to visit a sick man, Luther said: " No! By my body, no! Priests must not flee too soon, for it makes the people fearful. But, as has been said, we should spare the clergy and not load them down at the time of the plague, and when one is taken away another should be provided to visit the sick. In like manner we should not shun priests at the time of the plague, as we see people do. It is good not to burden all with the duties of visiting the sick but to select one or two. If the lot fell to me I should not avoid it. I have survived three plagues and visited several persons who had it, such as Schadewald, who had two plague spots which I touched. But it did not hurt me, thank God! Afterwards when I returned home I took up Margaret, who was then a baby, and put my unwashed hands on her face, but it was because I had forgotten; otherwise I should not have done it, which would have been tempting God."

QUESTIONS

Asked by a young margrave why he wrote so vehemently, Luther replied: "Our Lord God must first let fall a good hard thunder shower, then a fine gentle rain, and thus the ground is thoroughly moistened. Again, I can divide a little willow stick with my knife, but for a hard oak one needs an axe and wedge and even then can hardly split it."

When a letter was received asking whether it was permissible to baptize with warm water, the doctor answered: "Tell the ninny that water is water, whether it is cold or warm."

When Luther was asked whether it was better to fight against the enemy or to exhort, teach and raise up the infirm, he replied: "Both are good and necessary. To comfort the weak is certainly somewhat greater, although those who fight are improved by battling with adversaries. Either one is a gift of God. 'He that teacheth, let him wait on teaching, or he that exhorteth, on exhortation.' "[1]

On one occasion I[2] asked Doctor Luther: "My dear doctor, how does it happen that one imagines such dreadful things when one

[1] Romans, xii, 7–8.
[2] Schlaginhaufen, who noted this conversation in 1532.

hears a noise or is otherwise disturbed during the night, when commonly the very worst fears occur to one?" Doctor Martin replied: "The devil does it. Thieves, burglars and murderers are at work then, hence one cannot think of anything good. If we lived fine Christian lives, then we should have pleasant thoughts."

Luther was asked: "Since all men were damned on account of Adam's fall, why are not all saved through Christ? Why do many remain irreligious?" "That question," he said, "is inexplicable. It can be and ought to be answered only by a positive statement. When the query is urged: Why is God so exasperated with anger against human beings that he rejects them all at once and gives them over to condemnation? the reply should be made that he is not angry, because he gave his only begotten Son as a price for us, which proves that he does not wish to destroy or to condemn.

"If, moreover, it is asked, Why does God permit men to rush to destruction? you should ask in reply, Why did God give his own Son over unto death? For is not the latter a more certain indication of love than the former is of hate? True it is indeed that Satan deceived Adam, but on the other hand consider that soon after the fall Adam received the promise concerning the woman's seed.[1] We may estimate therefore, from his mission, how great is the goodness of the Father towards the world, which on so many accounts is most wicked."

"Accordingly we should not look to see how many evils and sins, how many miseries and calamities of all kinds, our human nature is subject to and how many are condemned for their wickedness, for God could have prevented all those things, if he had never created us or the world; but rather we should consider this, that God has willed that all things be thus accomplished. Let his will therefore stand for a reason.[2] And do not obtrude that satanic *Wherefore* into divine matters! God is not pleased with such questions nor is he able to endure them with equanimity, since he is Lord and administrator of all things, and wishes to arrange all in accordance with his wisdom. For not even a man would take in good part such questions from another man. In order, however, that we may be certain concerning the will of God, as to who are to be saved and who are not to be saved, he has willed

[1] Gen. iii, 15.
[2] Juvenal's Satires, vi, 223.

that this be made known to us through his
Word, when he said: ' He that believeth and
is baptized shall be saved; but he that believeth not, shall be damned.'[1] In conclusion, we must believe that God is by far
the best and most beneficent being, who accomplishes things which not only no man
does, but which no man is able to do. That
he sometimes, however, does things which
strike us as unreasonable, and are beyond
our comprehension, is not a matter for us to
inquire into; it is enough for us to know that
he does nothing without a fixed purpose.
But to go beyond that and anxiously investigate the counsels or works of the divine
Majesty, would be like trying to measure
the wind with a bushel, or to weigh fire with
scales."

When Luther was asked why God had
created flies and other evils infinite in number, which do so much harm to man and
other creatures, whereas we read in Genesis:
" And God saw everything that he had made,
and behold, it was very good," he replied:
" Whatever God has made is good in itself,
and if we had remained in the innocence of
Adam, we should have been able to play with
adders and snakes as we do with friendly

[1] Mark xvi, 16.

dogs and cats. But after the transgression and fall of Adam all things were made troublesome and harmful to us. For God cursed the ground and said: 'Thorns and thistles shall it bring forth to thee.' The pronoun *thee* spoils all; they can serve us no more, for their power to do so has been removed."

Peter Weller said: " It is an amazing thing that God is so powerful and yet does not make all men good." Luther replied: " Dear friend, go up to heaven and ask God why it is. Yet on the earth, in all God's works, you may see that he is wise, powerful and good."

Elizabeth, the wife of Dr. Cruciger, asked Luther: " What ought a pious and Christian man to do if in a church of the papists he should see the mass celebrated or the sacrament of the body and blood elevated by the priest? " Luther replied: " My dear Elsa, snatch not the priest from the altar nor put out the candles! If I were in a church of theirs at the elevation of the sacrament, I should raise my hands just as the rest did. I should adore it in reverence, because it is a true sacrament, since all the substantial elements are present. Particularly the great mass as celebrated by the papists is right, for the priest consecrates it, and besides it has the general approval of the church. It is otherwise with the private mass, which is no mass at all; it is not known whether the priest consecrates it, nor is it supported by the public profession of the church as a whole. Naaman, the Syrian, was permitted by Elisha to go with his king into the temple where idols were being worshiped, and St. Sebastian was willing to keep his faith hidden, unless questioned. Therefore it is quite allowable for you to be present at the celebration of their sacraments, provided you do not in your mind approve of their impieties."

Master Hyneck[1] questioned Luther as follows: "Doctor, if I had some Hungarian gold pieces or other treasure which I was unwilling to expend, and some one should come to me for a loan, would it be possible with a good conscience to refuse him and say that I had no money?" The doctor replied that this could be done with a good conscience, for in saying that he had no money, he would mean that he had none to lend. "John indeed says: 'But whoso hath this world's goods, and seeth his brother

[1] Hyneck is a pet name used for Ignatius, in this case Ignatius Perknowsky, one of Luther's boarders.

have need, and shutteth up his bowels of compassion from him, how dwelleth the love of God in him?'[1] and Christ also says: 'Give to him that asketh thee,'[2] meaning to him that is in real need; he does not say: 'Give to every idle and prodigal person,' yet these are commonly the greatest beggars, and although one gives them a great deal, they are not helped thereby. There is no needy person in this city, aside from the students. The poverty in the city is great but the laziness is still greater; hardly any of the poor can be induced to work for money, yet they will all beg. There is no real government here. For Christian[3] and Paceus[4] there is nothing that one can do; if I could help them, I wouldn't: the more one helps them the worse off they are. I am not going to take food from my wife and children and give it to those who will not be helped by it. Certainly the needy ought to be provided for; and if any one is really in need, I will aid him heartily in proportion to my ability. Nor ought any one to inter-

[1] 1 John iii, 17.

[2] Matthew, v. 42.

[3] An unidentified student.

[4] Probably Valentine Hartung, at this time (1532) deacon in Leisnig. On March 5 of the following year Luther wrote to the elector in his behalf. DeWette, *Luthers Briefe*, iv, 438.

pret superstitiously the passage: 'He that hath two coats, let him impart to him that hath none.'[1] For in the Scriptures one coat means all the clothing which any one needs, according to one's position and the demands made upon one, just as by bread is meant all the food which the body requires; thus a coat is the entire vesture. The devil, however, would gladly make new monks of us again by these superstitions, and give to the impious and idle the opportunity to live in luxury. At one time all those about me wanted to get rich, and there was no end of begging."

When asked how the evangelists[2] were able to write down what Christ said in the garden before the passion, when not all of them were present, and the three who were there were also asleep, the doctor replied: "Do you not think that Christ told them this after the resurrection, when he lived with them yet forty days? O, he no doubt told them many a good thing besides! Also the prayer which he made was certainly longer, for he prayed about half an hour, and many an argument must have occurred to him."

[1] Luke iii, 11.

[2] Matthew xxvi, 39; Mark, xiv, 35; Luke, xxii, 41.

Then some one else asked him: "How could the apostles sleep, since anxiety prevents sleep?" He replied: "Oh, the disciples had no special anxiety. They pitied him when they observed what he was doing, but sleep overcame them. As when several people watch by the side of a sick person; they condole with him, but they often fall asleep, while it is impossible for him to sleep. Therefore he comes three times and asks them to awake: 'Only do not sleep! To think that you do not even speak with me!' Ay, that is a great weakness in Christ, that he should ask help of those whom he has created! No human heart can realize what he must have suffered, when he sweated blood. Those were our sins that he bore."

Some one said: "Doctor, what ought I to do when I find men in my church, as I do sometimes, who have abstained from the sacraments for twenty years?" "Let them go to the devil!" replied the Doctor. "And if they die, then lay them on the flaying-place!" After a pause, the question was asked: "Should they even be compelled to come to the sacrament?" "By no means!" answered Luther. "That is the way of the papists. Just speak to them!" And he added: "I wonder why they stay away so much from the sacraments. Perhaps they are afraid of private confession."

Some one asked: " If a priest absolved a woman, who had killed her child, and the affair had been bruited about by others, ought the priest also, if asked, to testify concerning the matter before the judge? " "Not at all," said the doctor, for " the civil court and the court of conscience are to be kept distinct. That woman has confessed nothing to me, but to Christ. But if Christ is silent, I ought to be silent and simply deny that I had heard anything. If Christ has heard anything, let him tell it. I would, however, say to the woman privately during absolution: ' You whore, don't ever do that again! ' " — " Doctor, what if the woman herself should say that she had been absolved by you, and should claim her freedom on the ground that Christ had dismissed her? Are the judges, therefore, competent to pass upon the case? " Luther replied: " I say again that the two courts are to be kept separate. And if I were cited in this matter again, I would refuse, for I am not the man to talk and give testimony in a civil court, but in a court of conscience. Therefore I should say: If she is absolved, I, Doctor Martin, know nothing about it, but Christ, with whom she has spoken, to whom she has, or has not, confessed something, knows; he certainly knows whether he has absolved her or not; I know nothing about it, for it is not I, but Christ, that hears confession."

When a question was raised concerning matrimonial matters and the conversation fell upon the case of Hannah Moniana the doctor said that she was legally freed from Corbianus, since she was twenty-three years old and of age. "For guardians haven't so much power as parents over their children. Otherwise the theologian would either refuse flatly to consider marriage cases as belonging properly to the magistracy, or if urged, deliver his opinion in accordance with our doctrine: The consent of the parents is required, and clandestine engagements may be dissolved by the parents, but not by the guardians, other things being equal; but if the parties are unwilling to yield to this, the pastor is not bound by public law to defend his judgment, for it is not the pastors who have executive power, but the public magistrates." To this Luther added: "If Anna Strauss[1] should marry some one, and I should think the marriage not for her advantage, I should send her to her relatives;

[1] Luther's foster-daughter.

I should not dissolve the engagement. As, moreover, sons ought not to marry without consent, so the father ought not to compel them to, especially a step-father his step-son or step-daughter. No one ought to give judgment, except a judge; a preacher is not a judge, therefore he ought not to give judgment."

Asked whether a marriage contracted without religious rites was valid, and being told that certain of the older priests were desirous of contracting marriage in this way, Luther replied: " It doesn't matter, even if there is no religious ceremony, provided there are three good men present as witnesses including a priest and a deacon! It is then considered a marriage. And this should also be added: Let them not deny it! But when they are asked, let them freely confess! It is then a valid marriage."

Asked which was higher among the Jewish people, the priesthood or the authority of the state, he replied: " O, the priesthood! For that has to do with God while political affairs are the concern of men. The church is always more than the state." Asked again by the same person whether God really answered the high priest from the sanctuary, he replied: " O yes! Nothing is more certain. And if he heard the prayer of the priest, there appeared the flame or fire of God, which is called the Urim Thummim;[1] this was a sign that the prayer was heard. But when the flame did not appear, it was a sign that the prayer had not been heard."

[1] Exodus xxviii, 30.

36. MISCELLANEOUS.

" The church is an assembly of people depending on things that are not seen, and cannot be grasped with the senses, namely on the Word. Such an assembly believes what it professes without any addition, and thanks God for revealing the truth to us. The godless see nothing in the church (for it irks and pains them with its punishments) except sin and weakness, which offends them. They see the vices of the church members but not the honor and glory of the church."

" Wealth is the least important of all things upon the earth, the smallest gift that God has bestowed on man. What is it, compared to the Word of God? Yes, what is it, compared even to bodily gifts and beauty? What is it, compared to the gifts of the mind? Yet people strive so for it! By no category of logic can it be called good — for its substance, its quality, as a means or as an end. Therefore God gives it commonly to coarse fools, to whom he means no good."

Luther: " I wish I had all that I have written." *Major:* " One could then see, doctor, how your teaching grew." *Luther:*

" Yes, truly. At first I was weak, in many things very weak."

" I greatly delight in the stories of Terence and read him every night. . . . The *Hecyra* is a fine comedy, the best of the author, but, because it has no action it does not please the common student. But it is full of grave, sententious sayings, useful for common life, such as, ' All mothers-in-law hate their daughters-in-law.' That is a great curse but one can do nothing about it. I have seen many examples of it, as for instance at Eisenach, when a mother-in-law spat in the face of her daughter-in-law. The young women and her friends were so good that they said: 'What can we do? She is our mother?' And thus with patience they bore all their parents' injuries.

" Building a church is not instituting ceremonies, as wiseacres think, but freeing consciences and strengthening faith."

" A sleeping person resembles very much a dead one; it was therefore fitting to picture sleep as the brother of death, and to see in the day and night the image of life and death."

" Among writers I hate none so much as Jerome; he has only the name of Christian. He writes on fasts and virginity but nothing of faith. Dr. Staupitz, his diligent pupil, said: ' I should be pleased to know why he was canonized.' And Proles, Staupitz's predecessor in the vicariate, said: ' Truly I should not wish to have Jerome for prior, he is so strange."

" Jerome is a babbler like Erasmus; he tried to talk big and did not succeed. He promises the reader something but gives nothing. I wonder, too, at that time, hardly three hundred years after Christ, when the tongues were so well understood, there was such blindness in the Church. Augustine is a reasoner who will know and not merely imagine, and he teaches something. He is the best theologian who has written since the apostles, but we monks read not him but Scotus."

" It is a special plague of the devil that we have no certain legends of the saints, and it is strange what shameful things are in them. It is a hard labor to correct the legends." Then he read of St. Catharine[1] and said: " This contradicts all Roman history. Maxentius was drowned at Rome in the Tiber and never went to Alexandria, but Maximius was there (see Eusebius). Since

[1] St. Catharine of Egypt, according to the legend daughter of the king of that country.

the time of Cæsar and long before there had been no king in Egypt. It must have been a desperate villain who vexed Christendom with such lies: he must certainly sit low in hell. Such stories we once believed and would not have dared to contradict had we known the truth. Therefore, young men, thank God that you don't have to believe such things, or worse, now."

Melanchthon said to Luther: "Our emperor will live till 1548."[1] Luther replied: "The world won't last so long, for Ezekiel says it won't. . . . The end is at hand, at the very threshold. Let him who will do anything begin it betimes. The joys of the world are played out. The old peasants before Vienna think: 'Ah! Lord God, the Turks will subdue us!' Everything changes. If I were to enter my father's house it would look very different to me from what it did formerly. The best thing that ever came out of my father's property is that he brought me up. No money is ever better spent than in education."

"The common life of the Waldenses is without doubt the best, at least externally. They have many correct doctrines like ours;

[1] Melanchthon made this calculation on the basis of astrology.

they reject the mass, purgatory and the invocation of saints. They have a celibate priesthood, but a minister may marry when he chooses if he resigns his office. We should have been obliged to have the same rule, did we not allow married pastors, for otherwise how could we have gotten any? The Waldenses are diligent and temperate; they tell the truth and love their neighbors, and have an excellent system of teaching, but not the article of justification by faith, although they confess that men are saved by faith and grace. But they understand faith as the king of virtues and explain it as something different from our grace."

On the evening of April 3, 1538, the Prince of Anhalt, the elector's commissary, asked Luther to hunt with him the next day, and then to dine at his house. Luther answered: " I have been sent for this very purpose, but I am not a great chaser of the deer; I hunt the pope, cardinals, bishops, canons and monks."

" It is almost impossible for lawyers to be saved and difficult even for theologians. Most of the latter are now on the way to salvation, but Zwingli and Œcolampadius missed it. . . . They were in the same temptation as the papal lawyers, of saying:

' I have done wrong, therefore I am damned.'
Their speculative science tells them that
damnation is the reward of sin.   But theology
is a practical not a speculative science.
Zwingli never believed, his whole life long,
that Christ was really in the sacrament,
except in a spiritual, speculative sense."

" The wicked and the damned will be
under the earth on the last day, and while
they will see, in some way, the glory of the
blessed, they will be all the more tormented
by the sight."

December 16, 1536, during exceedingly
cold weather which had lasted for a week,
there came a flash of lightning followed by
a terrific crash of thunder. Astronomers
call this a *chasma* and say that it indicates
dryness of the atmosphere. Luther and
Bugenhagen both heard it, each in his own
home, and afterwards they discussed the
question whether these wonderful portents
signified anything, for it was quite unnatural
that we near the arctic circle should experience such portents as might be expected in
Africa, Asia and places near the tropics,
and they concluded that they were plainly
satanical. " I am of the opinion," said
Luther, " that the devils were planning to
hold a debate, when some angel interposed

this *chasma* and thus tore up their propositions. But the world pays no heed to such
infinite signs. When Franz von Sickingen
was about to die a similar crash was heard by
Philip Melanchthon, and one night Adolph,
an assistant of Lucas Cranach the painter,
when he set out with a peasant for Torgau,
saw in the sky a great star, near which was
a man beating a drum, and then in a vision
dreadful to behold he saw the Lord of hosts
in conflict with an opposing army. In
1516 the Elector John saw at Weimar a
great red star which seemed to turn first into
a candle, then into a cross, then into a yellow
star, and finally seemed to break in pieces.
This was witnessed in the year before the
Evangelical religion arose, and I apply it
to the progress of our faith, which arose red,
then burned as it bore the cross of persecution, then was dimmed with schism and now
remains a fixed star. But I attach no certain meaning to these signs which for the
most part are deceptive and satanical.
Many such omens have been seen in the last
fifteen years, all egregiously disregarded by
the skeptics. Let us await God's wrath
calmly. Our neighbor[1] has said, quite in

[1] From a note on the margin of the manuscript Kroker infers
that the reference is to Henry the Younger, Duke of Brunswick-Wolfenbüttel.

the manner of Epicurus: 'I can know nothing, I have learned nothing.' But he knows how to oppress the people and gather in their money."

"Martin Cellarius, an impious scoundrel, wishing to deceive me by adulation, said that my vocation was greater than that of the apostles. But I said: 'What am I compared to the apostles!'"

"A sacrament is a human action with divine promises, or a visible sign with promises."[1]

Peter Weller[2] said that the people of Esthland were simply Scythians, with bad morals and no buildings, sleeping, baking and living in ovens, looking like the devil. Dr. Luther answered: "Don't lie yourself to death, Peter! You can still be a lawyer."

"I have preached here twenty-four years, and have gone the way to church so often, that it is a wonder that I have not worn out my feet on the plaster as well as my shoes. I have done my part, and feel

---

[1] This is the general definition of "sacrament" which Luther set forth in his *Babylonian Captivity*, of 1520. *Cf.* Smith, *Life and Letters of Martin Luther*, p. 89. Augustine's definition, adopted by most churches, is "the outward and visible sign of an inward and spiritual grace." But Luther's definition is substantially in accordance with Aquinas, *Summae Theologiae Pars III*, Quaestio 6, art. 3.

[2] A student of jurisprudence at Wittenberg. Esthland is on the Gulf of Finland.

satisfied. If only I had preserved the letters sent to me, I should have filled a great house. The number of these letters is the testimony to my labor. But nothing has hurt me more than worrying, especially at night."

"Tomorrow I must lecture on the drunkenness of Noah, so that I must drink enough tonight to know what I am talking about, and experience its evil." Dr. Cordatus said: "By no means! You ought to do the contrary." Then Luther: "We must make the best of the vices peculiar to each country. The Bohemians gorge, the Wends[1] steal, the Germans swill right heartily. How then, dear Cordatus, would you beat a German except by making him drunk especially one who does not love music and women?"[2]

When he heard that his books were in the elector's library he said: "By no means let my books be put into the library, particularly the first ones, written in the beginning, which offend not only my adversaries but me also."

By way of farewell, Luther said to some

[1] The ancient population of Saxony.

[2] This is the nearest Luther ever came to the verse commonly attributed to him:

Who loves not women, wine and song,
He lives a fool his whole life long.

This verse appears first in a book called *Wandsbecker Boten* printed in 1775.

one: " Just tell our Lord God to be good, and we will fix everything all right."

" Games of cards and dice are very frequent, for this age has invented various games. It is so good at cheating! When I was a youth all games were forbidden, so that makers of cards and pipers were not allowed to go to the sacrament, and people were forced to confess if they had played a game, danced or attended an exhibition of juggling. But now these diversions are in high favor, and are defended on the ground that they exercise the natural powers."

" The Italians love the High Germans, whom they call ' Almanni alti,' but not the ' Almanni bassi,' i. e., Dutchmen and Belgians, for they are crafty and are worse than the Italians, according to the proverb: ' An Italian German is the devil incarnate.' "[2]

On April 1 (1538), he sat at home, speaking of the rigid diet prescribed by physicians, by which many men starved themselves to death. " It is true," said he, " that good diet is the best medicine for anyone who can stand it, but to live hygienically is to live miserably." Then he narrated several tales of people who had starved themselves to

[1] This proverb is interesting because Roger Ascham says that he heard it in Italy in the 16th century, but of "Italianate Englishmen."

death by the advice of physicians. "I eat
what I can, and die when God wills. 'Time
slips by and we grow old with the silent
years.'[1] When I think of my contemporaries,
men of fifty, how thin their numbers are![2]
Almost every thirty years brings a new age.
We all belong to the earth, and cannot escape
from it."

"When they crown an emperor at Trier,
they roast for him a whole ox, within the ox
a pig, within the pig a goose, within the goose
a fowl, within the fowl a bird."

Said Luther: "Would that I and all my
children were dead! For things in this world
are coming to a strange state. Whoever
shall live there, will see that things are constantly getting worse. Therefore our Lord
God is now taking his own away, and is
proving what John the Baptist says: 'His
fan he will take in his hand.'[3] He is now
gathering his wheat into the bushel, and into

[1] Ovid, *Fasti*, vi, 771.
[2] The Dominican, A. M. Weiss: *Lutherpsychologie als
Schlussel zur Lutherlegende*, Mainz, 1906, translated these
words "how thin they are!" and added: "apparently Luther
considered a barrel-like figure as a special beauty, or a great
blessing," p. 188. For this he was criticized by Preserved
Smith in the *American Historical Review*, January, 1910,
p. 369. The Jesuit Grisar now admits that the translation
given here is the correct one, and that this passage cannot
be used as a proof of Luther's gluttony. *Luther*, vol. ii,
1911, p. 246.
[3] Matt. iii, 12.

the garner, but with the chaff he will proceed in a wonderful manner: ' He will burn them with unquenchable fire,' says the text. That is what he did with Rome. First the righteous people had to die by the sword, but afterwards he came and smashed the government to pieces, so that people have been trying, even to the present day, to patch up the city, and the pope too has tried, and is trying yet, but they are unable to put it in order again. Thus he will proceed with Germany also, he will take away the upright, and then make an end of the German land, for it has well deserved the punishment and still continues its downward course. The Margrave[1] has now dismissed Alber[2] because he wrote to him in camp begging him not to burden the poor preachers with such heavy dues, for out of their salary from which they must support themselves they had to pay various taxes. Now he must be called a disturber of the peace! In addition to this his own fellow-citizens have hung a pair of shoes on his house, together with the inscription: ' Arise and walk!'[3] For such

---

[1] Joachim II, Margrave of Brandenburg, who had marched in the previous summer (1542) into Hungary against the Turks.

[2] Erasmus Alber, a personal friend of Luther.

[3] Matt. ix, 5.

contempt of the divine word and the ministers ought not God to strike out with his fists?"

"However, if we preachers got together and were united, as are the papists, then we would have just as little trouble. But that is the worst, that the preachers themselves are not a unit. Yet it would not be good and must be as it is, for it would perhaps result, as it has in the papacy, that the priests would again get control of the government. So it has ever been from the beginning of the world, that the preachers themselves have not been in agreement with each other. Alas, young friends! There is yet a sad time coming, and you will see it. Perhaps there may not be very much danger of it yet for fifty years, on account of our doctrine, since the youth of the present have been educated therein, but after that the people must look out! Therefore no one should be afraid now of the plague, but should only be glad to die. Alas, why fear death? Since Jesus Christ, the son of God, had to die, that may indeed be called death! Our death is nothing in comparison with that. And we know also that it does not harm us. Paul says: 'Christ died, and we shall all die.'"[1]

[1] II Cor. v, 14.

" The Lord's prayer binds the people to-gether and to one another, in that one prays for the other and with the other, and therefore it becomes strong and powerful, so that it dispels all evils and even death itself."

When mention was made of the blind Bernard Zettler, some one said: " It is to be hoped that his wife will get well, but he might as well be dead." Luther replied: " Alas, we must have the poor, the poor![1] Who knows whence we derive benefit? I have also in my house many useless folk. God has other thoughts than we. Who knows what benefit we obtain therefrom? Lazarus lay also before the door of the rich man, and perhaps half the country profited thereby. It is God's will that we have the poor among us, therefore we should support them, and I must see how we can provide for him, for he is nevertheless honest and he prays gladly and diligently, and he is training up his children finely."

" God exalts the humble," said Schiefer, " Philip was born in a peasant's hut." Luther replied: " It is God's pleasure to exalt the humble and put down the mighty from their seats. There is no court in which there is not

---

[1] The repetition of a word or phrase for emphasis is character-istic of Luther's familiar talk.

some poor person, upon whose advice the
prince depends. Chancellor Francis Burkart
has precedence over all the nobles, and the
same is true of Chancellor Brück; and I,
though born in a country place, sometimes
share in the greatest councils. And consider:
in all Meissen among so many nobles there
are scarcely two who are fitted to rule! It
takes big men to administer a government,
men of noble talents, who do not act as do the
princes and bishop of Passau. The genius
of Alexander was tried by the cares of government. But God raises up genius from the
common people. But this is the worst,
that sometimes these humble folk learn to be
haughty, like Agricola and Schenk; then the
devil is to pay and their fall is swift."

When mention was made of the three sons
of the old man Brück, I[1] said: "The old
man was poor." "Very poor," said the
doctor, "at first, but afterwards he left
Doctor Gregory Brück wealth amounting to
about 4000 gulden. But God is wont to
exalt the sons of paupers, as he has brought
even me, the son of extremely poor parents,
to this position." Behold the life of Luther!

"If you would learn how to conquer the
greatest, most dreadful and shameless ene-

[1] Mathesius, 1540.

mies, that otherwise might overwhelm you and do you harm in both body and soul, and against whom you would need to buy all kinds of arms and pay out all your money to learn to use them; then know there is a sweet, lovely little herb, whose name is Patience. Yes, you will say, but how can I find this medicine? The answer is this: Take for yourself the faith that no one can harm you, except it be the will of God! But should you suffer harm, it will result from the friendly, gracious will of God in such a way that the enemy will do a thousand times more harm to himself than to you; whence arises the love which says: Therefore will I do him good in return for evil, and heap coals of fire on his neck. These are the arms with which we win over the enemies that seem like great mountains, which do not rush upon us and are not to be overcome by iron and steel. Love teaches us patience."

" Things[1] are our teachers. He who does not know things, is unable to draw forth the sense from words. Wherefore Münster[2] often errs, since he does not know things. I have explained more texts through the knowledge

[1] The Latin word translated *things* throughout this passage is *res*, which has a wide variety of meanings.

[2] Sebastian Münster issued a translation of the Bible in 1534.

of things, than through the knowledge of grammar. If lawyers did not know things, no one would understand their words. Wherefore it is the study of things that achieves results."

" I am able to write letters, but not in a Ciceronian and oratorical style, as Agricola does; but I have substance, although Latin words and elegance fail me."

He consoled a woman named Selmenitz, when she was ill, as follows: " We have waited much too long, when we first seek to know Christ in the last hour of need. He came to us in baptism and has remained with us, and has made us a fine bridge upon which we may go from this life through death to the life beyond. That you ought certainly to believe!"

" Aside from man no being cries except the dog and the crocodile; and the latter for the most part only makes believe. Tears are born in the heart, and ascend to the eyes, since when one weeps, the whole heart is moved."

" Jerome[1] wishes to make much of his old sciences, but we of today are much wiser. If your son[2] were twenty years old, I could

[1] Jerome Schurff, an eminent jurist and colleague of Luther. See Koestlin, *Martin Luther, sein Leben und seine Schriften*[5], 1903, Bd. ii, S. 468–471, or *Luther's Correspondence*, i, p. 543.
[2] The son of Justus Jonas, aged 14.

teach him in three hours the whole vocabulary
of the Sophists,[1] together with the thought.
It has cost us a great deal to learn those
things thoroughly, but today many things in
addition can be learned from the dialectic
of Melanchthon."

"This book should not be called Terence,
but the comedies of Scipio and Laelius,[2]
for an African could not speak such pure
Latin, nor could a man not well versed in
affairs express such opinions. But Laelius
and Scipio were trained in wars, politics and
household affairs; they were able to express
weighty judgments. And if there were not so
many wise sayings in the works of Terence,
they would have perished long ago. Hans
Metzsch[3] is portrayed in Thraso, and in that
scene where Thraso stormed the castle of
Thais,[4] Scipio[5] ridiculed those soldiers who
boast at home, but when it comes to real
fighting are worthless. I delight greatly in
the plays of Terence, and read in his works
every night."

[1] By Sophists Luther meant the Schoolmen.

[2] Modern scholars give little weight to the old charge made
by Terence's rivals, that he had been assisted in the writing
of his plays by his friends Scipio and Laelius. In the prologue
to the *Adelphi* he alludes to the charge, but says that he regards it as complimentary to himself.

[3] Bailiff of Wittenberg, see *supra* p. 46.

[4] Terence, *Eunuchus*, Act iv, Scene 7.

[5] Scipio assumed as author of Terence's plays.

" I have three bad dogs: ingratitude, pride, envy. Whom the three dogs bite, is very sorely bitten."

" It is evident that the stars were not created in vain, for they mark the seasons, years, months, days and nights, and they protect the crops. But we neglect the certain uses of the stars and seek uncertain ones. So it goes with those who add to or take from the Word of God."

Some one said: " Doctor, miners give liberally, but they have this vice: on Sundays and Saturdays they get drunk." Luther replied: " Miners of course ought not to do that, but if they are diligent the other days, one must allow them something. One must not bluntly refuse them, or they would become still more unruly. Their work is very severe and accompanied by extreme danger, and the climate should be considered. I drink too, but not every one should imitate me, for all do not bear my labors. If therefore the miners hear the morning sermon and pray, then in view of their labors and customs one should not notice their absence from the afternoon service."

" The world has not existed long; if people had lived as long as Adam, six generations would have reached to the present. But before God the time has been still shorter, for in his sight a thousand years are but as one day."[1]

" The world's history I divide into six ages: the ages of Adam, Noah, Abraham, David, Christ and the pope. Each of the first five lasted approximately a thousand years. The age of the pope may be reckoned as beginning about 5000 years after the creation of the world, that is, when Hildebrand[2] publicly forbade the marriage of priests under Henry IV. At that time St. Bernard was born. But the pope will not complete his millennium."

" This life is preliminary to the future life. But if God adorns with such innumerable gifts this mean, corrupt life, what will he do for the future life, when sin will cease and eternal justice flourish? "

" It is strange that men are so heedless and arrogant, when there are on every hand such a multitude of reasons for being humble. The hour of death is uncertain, nor is the food we eat within our control, nor the sun and air by which we live, nor the day, nor sleep, to say nothing of spiritual things, such as the public and private sins by which we are op-

[1] Ps. xc, 4.
[2] Pope as Gregory VII, 1073–1085.

pressed. But our hearts are adamantine, without a care for anything."

Luther told of the avarice of a certain woman, who, since she feared that the end of the world prophesied by Stieffel[1] was at hand scattered her money about in her room, saying: "You cursed mammon, you shall not be my master!" Afterwards, when the day fixed by Stieffel had come and gone, she gathered up the money and hid it again, and gave not a penny to help the poorest person.

"A man once hired an ass to ride. The owner of the ass went on foot alongside the rider. But when it became too hot upon the ass for the rider, he requested the other to ride, while he himself walked in the shade alongside. This the master of the ass would not permit, for he had rented him the ass to ride, and not its shade; for the latter he must pay extra. This is a picture of the world, which gives nothing gratis to any one, not even a shady place."

On the day of Pentecost in the year 1540 Luther said at table: "I am now an old preacher, and have preached for twenty-eight years, ordinarily three times a Sunday, and once four times, when Duke Frederic

[1] Michael Stieffel, pastor in Lochau, had prophesied that the world would come to an end on a certain day in 1533. See *Tischreden*, Weimar Ed. III, 290.

was here." And to the same one he added: "For we young preachers are learned; God has given me moreover strength, otherwise I had not endured such great labors."

"I am able to boast that I am not so bad and angry towards any one as to wish him the eternal wrath of God, not even the bishop of Mainz, whom I have hated as being of all living persons most thoroughly a sceptic. I have not been so hostile to the Duke of Brunswick and Duke George. But they do not fear the wrath of God. Wherefore he is in no haste to punish them."

Luther said: "I intend to write sometime concerning the vices of all the countries. To the Germans I will assign drunkenness, to the Italians, deceitfulness, for they now surpass the Greeks with their lies." Melanchthon replied: "Almost all princes think nowadays that it is wise to resort to devious ways and practices, nor do the majority think it wrong for the great to resort to deception. But in regard to the Germans being fond of drink, there are two reasons for that: 1. They are intemperate on account of the coldness of the climate; wherefore the farther north men live, the more they drink. 2. The Germans are sociable. This causes them to indulge in the cup. Italy has no social clubs."

To Robert Barnes[1] Luther said: "You English have no wolves, because you are wolves yourselves."

"A child of seven years dies most joyfully without fear of death, but as soon as we adults feel ill, the sense of death and of hell begins, and we tremble at the thought of dying."

Luther, admiring the fruitfulness of the season, said: "Ah, who gives thanks for such great blessings? Our whole life ought to be nothing else but the praise of God. For what is life, without the praise of God?"

"My adversaries have made me learned. I cannot repay Eck for what he has taught me, and the pope cannot punish him enough, for he ruined his cause. If I were the pope, I would give Eck a cardinal's hat and then burn him."

The doctor said: "Agricola, the poor little man! What a pest is vainglory! I am only sorry for his wife and children. He wishes to be considered more learned than Master Philip and I, and we are not able to yield to him. He regards Bugenhagen as beneath him, but Bugenhagen is a great theologian, and has much energy. Doctor Creutziger

[1] An English Lutheran, originally an Augustinian who had studied at Oxford, who spent much time at Wittenberg. He was martyred by Henry VIII in 1540.

was always more learned than Agricola, and is a distinguished theologian."

Said Luther: " How I do hate people who lug in so many languages as Zwingli does; he spoke Greek and Hebrew in the pulpit at Marburg!" Schiefer added: " Hofmann at Jena does the same; he wrote eight books and hardly one is of any value."[1] " Philip was against him," remarked Luther.

Martin[2], a certain small man from Strassburg, not only compared Luther with the Apostles, but considered him in some ways superior to them. When told of this by Jonas,[3] the doctor replied: " O no! The Apostles were great, holy men. If God only permits me to be his fire-tender and stand behind the door! And I am not that yet by far."

Mention having been made of Scipio, Schiefer said: " We ought to have such a leader against the Turks!" The Doctor replied: " If we only had Abraham! He could send 4000 angels in advance, as when he killed four kings with the aid of his servants.[4] Ah, he was a great man and God's

---

[1] Reading *prodest* for *prodiit*.

[2] Cellarius; *cf. supra*, p. 233.

[3] Justus Jonas, a teacher at Wittenberg, a friend and frequent table-companion of Luther.

[4] Gen. xiv.

good friend. He trusted God well, so God stood honorably by him, although he had nothing of his own, and with so many people and cattle had to go upon other people's territory, like the ox-drivers."

"It is my firm belief that the angels are getting ready, putting on their armor and girding their swords about them, for the last day is already breaking, and the angels are preparing for the battle, when they will overthrow the Turks and hurl them, along with the pope, to the bottom of hell."

"The world will perish shortly. Among us there is the greatest ingratitude and contempt for the Word, among the papists there is slaughter and blasphemy. That will knock the bottom out of the barrel."

"As things are beginning to go, the last day is at the door, and I believe that the world will not endure a hundred years. For the light of the gospel is now dawning. That day will follow with thunder and lightning, for the voice of the Lord and of the trumpet are conveyed in the thunder. It will come from the east, and the earth will be severely shaken by the crash with such horror, that men will die of fear."

"I believe that the last day is not far off, for this reason: the gospel is now making its last effort, and it is just the same as with a light which, when it is about to go out, gives forth a great flash at the end as if it intended to burn a long time yet, and then it is gone. So it appears to be in the case of the gospel, which seems on the point of widely extending itself, but I fear that it also will go out in a flash, and that the last day will then be at hand. It is just so with a sick man: when he is about to die he often appears most refreshed, and in a trice he has departed."

BIBLIOGRAPHICAL NOTE.

D. Martin Luthers Werke, kritische Gesamtausgabe. Weimar. 1883ff. Tischreden, vols. i, ii and iii, 1912ff, edited by Ernst Kroker. (In course of publication; Volume i contains notes of Dietrich and Medler, 1531ff; volume ii, contains notes of Schlaginhaufen, 1531–2, of Rabe, 1532, and of Cordatus, 1531ff; volume iii, contains notes by Cordatus, Weller and Lauterbach, 1531-8.)

M. Anton Lauterbachs Tagebuch auf das Jahr 1538, herausgegeben von J. K. Seidemann. Dresden, 1872.

Luthers Tischreden in der Mathesischen Sammlung, herausgegeben von Ernst Kroker. Leipzig, 1903. (Contains notes by Mathesius, 1540, Heydenreich, 1542-3, Besold, 1544, Lauterbach, 1539.)

D. Martini Lutheri Colloquia, edita ab H. E. Bindseil. Lemgoviae et Detmoldiae, 1863-6. Three volumes. (Lauterbach's edition of the table talk.)

D. Martin Luthers Tischreden, herausgegeben von K. E. Förstemann und H. E. Bindseil. Berlin, 1844-8. Four volumes. (Aurifaber's edition of the table talk.)

BIBLIOGRAPHICAL NOTE

LUTHER'S TABLE TALK, a critical study, by Preserved Smith. New York, Columbia University Press, 1907. (Macmillan Co., agents.)

LIFE AND LETTERS OF MARTIN LUTHER, by Preserved Smith. Second edition, Boston, 1914.

LUTHER'S CORRESPONDENCE AND OTHER CONTEMPORARY LETTERS, translated and edited by Preserved Smith. Volume i, Philadelphia, 1913.

INDEX

INDEX

Comets, 102.
Common people, the, 127, 192, 240.
Commonplaces, Melanchthon's, 204.
Confession, 222, 223; of Augsburg, 204.
Constance, Council of, 142; city of, 197.
Constantinople, 21.
Copernicus, xvii, 104.
Corbianus, 223.
Cordatus, x, xxiv, 66, 192, 234.
Corpus juris, 6.
Cranach, Lucas, 232; the younger, 62.
Creation, 152; meaning of, 183.
Creed, the, 176.
Creutziger, 248.
Cromwell, Thomas, 79.
Crucifixion, the, 185.
Cruciger, 76.

Dabrun, 91.
Damned, the, 231.
Daniel, 200.
David, 76, 81, 98–100, 208.
Day, the last, 251.
Death, fear of, 238.
Decalogue, the, 176.
Demea, 3.
Demons, 158.
Demosthenes, 61, 184.
Deuteronomy, 178.
Devil, see Satan.
Devils, 133, 134.
Diet, 235.
Dietrich, Veit, xi, 67, 94.
Doctrine, the importance of, 197.
Dogs, 71, 244.
Dominicans, the, 151.
Donatists, the, 206.
Donatus, 2.
Dreams, 161, 162.
Dresden, 66.
Drunkenness among the Germans, 49, 72, 99, 234, 244, 247.
Dutchmen, the, 235.

Ecclesiasticus, 178.
Eck, J., of Trier, 35.
Eck, J., of Ingolstadt, 147, 248.
Eclipses, 103, 104.
Education, 3.
Egranus, 112, 113.
Egypt, 229.
Eisenach, 227.
Eisleben, 20.
Elbe, 202.
Elisha, 208, 218.

Elizabeth, Luther's daughter, ix.
Elizabeth, wife of Dr. Cruciger, 217.
Elizabeth, the mother of John the Baptist, 56.
Elsa, mistress of the Archbishop of Mainz, 74, 75.
Engagements, clandestine, 223.
England, opinion there concerning the Wittenberg reformers, 82; King of, 77, 85, 203.
Epicureanism (skepticism), 112, 118.
Epicureans, 140.
Epicurus, 120, 233.
Erasmus, 105, 106, 108, 109, 110, 111, 112, 114, 228; his *Colloquies, Catechism* and *Miscellany*, 107; his *Praise of Folly* and *Julius*, 108; his *Hyperaspistes*, 110; his *New Testament*, 111.
Erfurt, 5, 12, 13, 33; population of, 19.
Esthland, 233.
Eusebius, 228.
Eutzsch, 5.
Eve, 60.
Evil, problem of, 116, 117.
Excommunication, 145.
Exodus, the, 50.
Ezekiel, 7, 229.

Faber, J., 86.
Faith, 12; of younger people, 57; aided by reason, 115; nature of, 121.
Ferdinand, King of Hungary, 70, 86, 98, 138, 169.
Fleck, 24.
Fornicators, 157, 167.
Forster, 192.
France, 29; King of, 71, 81, 86, 139.
Franciscans, the, 151, 152, 155.
Frederic II, German Emperor, 148.
Frederic, Elector of Saxony, 29, 31, 53, 79, 93, 98, 106.
Friars, the, 146.
Future life, the, 89, 117, 122, 245.

Galatians, 178, 179.
Games, 235; gymnastic, 99.
Genesis, 62, 182.
George, Duke of Albertine Saxony, 36, 66, 70, 71, 83, 87, 98, 106, 116, 120, 169, 247.
Germans, the, 85, 199, 247.
Germany, 26, 29, 32, 86, 87, 161, 199, 237.

INDEX

INDEX

INDEX

INDEX